COLD-BLOODED BILLIONAIRE
NEGOTIATION TACTICS

HOW THE WORLD'S MOST RUTHLESS
DEALMAKERS CONTROL THE GAME

MARK McCLURE

Paperback ISBN: 979-8-9929288-0-8; Epub ISBN: 979-8-9929288-1-5

DISCLAIMER

1. Legal Disclaimer

"This book is for informational and educational purposes only. The strategies, case studies, and examples provided are based on publicly available information, historical accounts, and the author's personal experiences. While every effort has been made to ensure accuracy, the author and publisher make no guarantees regarding the outcomes of applying these strategies in real-world negotiations or business dealings. Readers are encouraged to consult with legal, financial, and business professionals before making any decisions based on the content of this book. The author and publisher disclaim any liability for the use or misuse of the information contained herein."

2. Ethical Considerations Disclaimer

"The tactics discussed in this book are drawn from real-world business strategies employed by some of the most successful negotiators in history. Some of these methods may be considered aggressive, unconventional, or controversial. This book does not endorse illegal, unethical, or manipulative business practices but aims to provide insight into how high-stakes negotiations are conducted at the highest levels. The reader is responsible for applying these strategies in a manner that aligns with their personal and professional ethics."

3. Case Study & Example Disclaimer

"The case studies, historical examples, and references to specific individuals or corporations in this book are based on publicly available information, personal experience, or widely known industry practices. Any opinions expressed about these individuals or businesses are the author's own and do not represent endorsements or statements of fact. Any similarities to private, non-public negotiations are purely coincidental."

4. Financial & Business Risk Disclaimer

"Negotiation and deal-making involve financial risk. There are no guarantees of success, and past results do not predict future outcomes. The strategies presented in this book may not be suitable for all individuals or business situations. The reader assumes full responsibility for any business decisions made based on the material provided."

5. Copyright & Reproduction Notice

6. Personal Responsibility Statement

"This book is intended to challenge conventional thinking and provide advanced negotiation strategies. However, success in business, negotiation, or deal-making depends on numerous factors, including market conditions, industry knowledge, timing, and personal skill. The author and publisher assume no responsibility for individual results or business outcomes

Table of Contents

CHAPTER 3:
Control Without Ownership – The Real Key to Wealth . .37

CHAPTER 4:
Information Asymmetry – Winning Before the
Other Side Knows the Game. 53

Introduction

For the past 35 years, I've been obsessed with billionaires (for lack of a better word)—not just their wealth, but how they bend deals to their will and walk away on top every single time.

I mean, think about it—what really separates the ultra-successful from everyone else in negotiations? It's not just deep pockets. If that were the case, why do some billionaires walk into a deal and absolutely destroy their competition while others lose their fortune?

The truth is, money is not the driving factor in the biggest negotiations. The real weapons? Cunning. Subterfuge. Absolute confidence. Cold-blooded strategy. A mastery of negotiation tactics that 98% of businesspeople never develop. These individuals play the game at an entirely different level, using power, influence, and psychological warfare in ways most people wouldn't even think of.

They Are Billionaires for a Reason

For decades, I've studied their every move—dissecting their deals, breaking down their negotiations, and most importantly, using these tactics myself. I've personally closed deals from $10K to over $100 million in more than 30 different industries across 4 continents, starting from nothing—literally nothing but a credit card as my capital at age 24.

But I don't need to sit here and brag about what I've done, who I've met, and the deals I've closed. If you want that information, go check my LinkedIn

https://www.linkedin.com/in/mark-mcclure-31b2858/
or visit my firm's website, *www.GenXCP.com*
(GenX Capital Partners)

The real foundation that has made all of this possible? My wife, Paula Rodriguez Wallem, who has been my rock. And most importantly, my Lord and Savior, Jesus Christ—without whom none of this would be possible.

Now Let's Pull Back The Curtain of "Cold Blooded Billionaire Negotiation Tactics" and Get A Glimpse What You Will Learn.

What I've uncovered over the last three decades is a brutal, battle-tested playbook—the exact strategies that the corporate raiders, private equity titans, and elite power players use every single day to control the game.

What you're holding isn't some "Negotiation 101" handbook. This is WAR STRATEGY for high-level dealmakers.

This is not about "win-win" garbage or mirroring body language like some amateur sales seminar. This is about dominating negotiations, outmaneuvering opponents, and structuring deals that leave YOU in control. Whether you're closing a multi-million-dollar real estate deal, negotiating a business takeover, or even working a high-stakes personal deal, these tactics will put you miles ahead of the competition.

What You'll Learn
in This KICK ASS Book

- ## How Billionaires Think & Manipulate Negotiations

  The psychology of elite dealmakers—how they see the world, what they prioritize, and the mind games they use to crush their opponents. Trust me, they don't think like the "Average Joe Entrepreneur."

- ## The Art of Leverage & Power

  Why controlling the power dynamic matters more than the actual deal terms—and how billionaires have MASTERED this skill to always walk away winning.

- **Mind-Blowing Case Studies**

  Real-world war stories of how business titans, tech moguls, and real estate sharks have used these strategies to obliterate their competition. These aren't just lessons—they're weapons you can use.

- **The Most Ruthless Closing Techniques**

  How billionaires manufacture urgency, remove every escape route, and force the other side into a "YES" on their terms. These are real, hard-hitting tactics that have closed billion-dollar deals behind closed doors.

- **How to Weaponize Time & Pressure**

  When to drag negotiations out to make the other side bleed... and when to speed things up to push them into bad decisions.

- **The Psychological Warfare Playbook**

  Strategies like the silent pause, the takeaway close, and manufactured scarcity—all designed to break the other side's will and make them fold.

This Might Be the Most Powerful Book on Negotiation Ever Written.

If you want to dominate the room, control the conversation, and make people agree to YOUR terms, this book is your weapon. Once you start reading, you won't be able to put it down. Now...

LET'S DIVE IN.

Mark McClure
Author
GenX Capital Partners
Managing Partner

CHAPTER 1:
The Billionaire Mindset –
Thinking Like Power Negotiator

Most people see negotiation as a conversation about price, terms, and compromise. Billionaires and top decision makers, however, approach it as a battle of leverage and control. They don't focus on winning just one deal; they structure agreements that give them the upper hand long after the contract is signed.

To negotiate like a billionaire, you need to shift your mindset from trying to get the best deal in the moment to ensuring that every deal sets you up for greater power, influence, and profits in the future.

Negotiation is a War of Leverage, Not Just Words

Most people also think negotiation is about being the best talker in the room, crafting the perfect argument, or outsmarting the other side with clever tactics. But billionaires and elite entrepreneurs know better. Negotiation isn't won with words—it's won with **leverage**. That's right....leverage!

Leverage is what forces the other side to accept your terms, not because they agree with you, but because they have no better option. The best dealmakers don't spend time arguing over minor details or trying to persuade someone with logic. Instead, they structure situations where the other party has no choice but to concede.

Why Leverage Beats Persuasion Every Time

- **The person with fewer options loses.** If you're negotiating with only one possible outcome—whether it's selling a business, securing an investor, or closing a deal—you're at the mercy of the other side. But if you have multiple options, you can walk away and leave them scrambling.

- **Money talks but leverage screams.** Having deep pockets is great, but what really matters is controlling the terms. A billionaire can walk into a deal with less cash than their competitors and still win because they've structured the deal to their advantage *before negotiations even start*.

- **Control the situation, control the deal.** The best negotiators manipulate deadlines, competition, and external pressures to make the other party feel like they have no choice but to accept the terms on the table.

How Billionaires Set Up Leverage Before the First Offer

Billionaire dealmakers don't wait until they're sitting across the table to think about leverage—they build it long before the first conversation.

- **They create alternatives.** If they're buying a company, they make sure they have multiple targets lined up so they're never desperate to close a deal. If they're raising capital, they pit investors against each other to drive up terms in their favor. More on this later.

- **They control information.** The less the other party knows about their actual position, the stronger their leverage. Keeping certain details private—or strategically leaking the right information—can shift the power balance.

- **They manufacture urgency.** Deadlines, competitive bidding, and media pressure can make the other party feel like they're running out of time, forcing them to agree before they fully assess the deal.

The most powerful negotiators **don't argue—they apply pressure**. When done right, the other side will convince themselves that your terms are the best option, not because you persuaded them, but because they see no other way forward.

Building Leverage Before the Negotiation Begins

The most skilled negotiators don't wait until they're sitting at the table to think about leverage—they set up the game long before the first conversation takes place. They create an environment where they have multiple options while ensuring the other side has limited choices. By the time negotiations officially begin, the other party is already in a position where they are more likely to accept the terms being offered.

- **Having alternatives is power.** If a negotiator walks into a deal with only one option, they are at the mercy of the other party. The best negotiators always have a backup plan—whether it's another investor, a competing acquisition target, or an alternative source of funding. This allows them to negotiate without fear, knowing that they can walk away if necessary.

- **Making the other side believe they have no better options.** The key to controlling leverage is making sure that, whether real or perceived, the other party believes their best outcome lies in making a deal with you. This can be done through market positioning, strategic alliances, or by influencing the competitive landscape before the negotiation begins.

- **Removing competing options.** Billionaires and top entrepreneurs use exclusivity agreements, preemptive acquisitions, and strategic partnerships to eliminate the other party's alternatives before they even realize it. By limiting their choices, they make it easier to dictate the terms of the deal.

When leverage is built in advance, the actual negotiation becomes a formality—one in which the powerful party dictates the terms while the weaker party is left trying to justify their own compromises.

Controlling the Timeline to Apply Pressure

Time is one of the most overlooked weapons in negotiation. The party that has the flexibility to wait almost always holds the upper hand. In contrast, the side that is rushing to close the deal or operating under a tight deadline is far more likely to accept unfavorable terms simply to move forward. Billionaires and elite negotiators don't just use time—they manipulate it to their advantage.

By strategically controlling the pace of the negotiation, top dealmakers create an environment where the other party begins to feel pressure, uncertainty, and urgency. When people feel time pressure, they become less rational, more reactive, and more willing to concede just to reach a resolution.

Real-World Example: How Steve Wynn Used Time Pressure to Secure Prime Land for His Casinos

Billionaire Steve Wynn, the mastermind behind some of Las Vegas's most iconic resorts, knew that controlling time in negotiations was just as important as controlling money. One of his most brilliant uses of time pressure came when he was securing prime real estate for the Wynn Las Vegas resort.

In the early 2000s, Wynn had his sights set on a highly valuable strip of land on the Las Vegas Strip, but the owners were holding out for a higher price, thinking he was desperate to acquire it quickly.

Instead of chasing the deal, Wynn deliberately slowed down negotiations, making it seem like he had other options, even publicly hinted at alternative locations, creating doubt in the sellers' minds about whether they would actually land the sale.

As time passed, the property owners started to feel the pressure. They were sitting on land that wasn't generating income, and there weren't many other buyers with Wynn's vision and financial backing. Meanwhile, the Las Vegas market was booming, and Wynn knew that if he waited long enough, they would start to worry about missing out on a massive payday.

Sure enough, after months of strategic stalling, the sellers cracked under the pressure—they agreed to sell the land to Wynn at a far lower price than they originally wanted. He walked away with the perfect location for his next mega-resort, and they walked away realizing they had just been outplayed.

Lesson: Wynn controlled time, not the seller. By making them feel urgency while showing no urgency himself, he forced them into a weaker position—and landed a once-in-a-lifetime deal on his terms.

The Side with the Deadline Loses

The party under the most external pressure is at a significant disadvantage in any negotiation. Whether it's a public company facing shareholder expectations, a CEO trying to close a deal before a quarterly earnings report, or a distressed seller needing fast liquidity, tight deadlines create desperation—which can be exploited.

- **Shareholder and investor pressure**. Public companies often face intense scrutiny from shareholders and investors. If a company needs to close a deal before an earnings call or a major investor meeting, a skilled negotiator can stall just long enough to make the other side anxious, increasing their willingness to accept weaker terms.

- **Loan maturities and financial obligations**. When a company has a looming debt payment, construction deadline, or financial obligation, it becomes increasingly willing to cut a deal just to stay afloat. Negotiators who recognize this can hold firm and extract better terms by letting the clock run out.

- **End-of-quarter and year-end pressures**. Corporate decision-makers are often under pressure to finalize deals by the end of a fiscal quarter or year. Knowing this, top negotiators drag out discussions, delay responses, and hold back approvals until the last minute—forcing the other side to scramble for a resolution, often making costly mistakes in the process.

Real-World Example:
How Amancio Ortega Exploited a Seller's Deadline to Buy Prime London Real Estate

Billionaire Amancio Ortega, the founder of Zara and one of Europe's richest real estate investors, has built a global empire by knowing exactly when to strike. One of his most effective negotiation strategies is waiting out sellers who are under financial pressure, then forcing them to accept his terms when they have no other options.

In 2019, Ortega set his sights on Admiralty Arch, a historic and highly coveted property in London. The building had been acquired by a luxury hotel developer that planned to convert it into an exclusive five-star hotel. However, as the project progressed, the developer ran into severe financial trouble—rising construction costs, delays, and growing investor pressure put them in a desperate position.

Ortega knew that the developer had no time to play hardball. Their investors were demanding results, their financing was running dry, and they were racing against deadlines to avoid a total financial collapse. Instead of jumping in with an aggressive bid, Ortega let the clock run down, watching as their options disappeared one by one.

Just when the developer was at their breaking point, Ortega stepped in with a lowball offer—one far below their initial asking price. But at that stage, they had no choice. With no time to secure alternative buyers and their financial backers demanding a resolution, they reluctantly accepted Ortega's terms.

By simply waiting out the clock, Ortega was able to acquire prime London real estate at a massive discount, proving once again that in high-stakes negotiations, the side with the dead-line always loses.

Lesson: Let Time Do the Work

Ortega didn't need to negotiate aggressively—he let the sell-er's desperation do the negotiating for him. When someone is under extreme time pressure, they become far more willing to make concessions they would never normally accept. The key is patience. If you can afford to wait, while the other side can't, you already have the upper hand

The ability to spot external pressures on the other party and apply controlled delay tactics can shift power dramatically. **Billionaires never negotiate on someone else's timeline—they create their own.**

Creating Artificial Urgency

Deadlines don't have to be real to be effective. Skilled negoti-ators manufacture urgency to make the other party feel like they must act immediately, even when they actually have more time than they realize. By creating the illusion of scarcity, competition, or exclusivity, they make people fear missing out—forcing them to agree to terms they would otherwise resist.

- **The "limited-time offer" strategy.** Setting artificial expiration dates on an offer forces the other party to make decisions faster than they normally would. Even if the deadline isn't set in stone, the fear of missing an opportunity creates a psycho-logical push to close the deal quickly.

- **Creating a competitive environment.** One of the most ef-fective ways to speed up decision-making is to introduce the idea of other interested buyers, investors, or partners. The fear that a competitor might take the deal instead can push the other party to act under pressure, often agreeing to less favorable terms.

- **Leveraging media and public perception**. Strategic leaks to the media or controlled public announcements can be used to generate external pressure on decision-makers. For example, if a company is considering an acquisition, leaking information about another potential buyer can create a sense of urgency that forces executives to make quicker, less calculated decisions.

In reality, the **"urgency"** is often an illusion—but the psychological impact is very real. When people **feel rushed**, they **prioritize speed over logic**—and that's when the best negotiators strike.

Using Silence and Delays Strategically

Silence is an underestimated negotiation tactic, but it is one of the most powerful. People naturally dislike uncertainty, so when faced with silence or unexpected delays, they begin to second-guess themselves. Billionaire dealmakers intentionally slow down negotiations at critical moments to make the other party feel off-balance, anxious, and more likely to chase the deal.

- **Deliberate response delays**. Instead of responding immediately, high-level negotiators pause for days or even weeks, letting the other side wonder what's happening. This creates doubt and insecurity, making them more likely to reach out again—often with better terms.

- **Avoiding instant counter offers.** When given an offer, less experienced negotiators feel the need to immediately respond. Top dealmakers do the opposite—they let the offer sit, knowing that silence alone can make the other party feel uncomfortable and more likely to sweeten the deal just to keep the discussion moving.

- **Using "ghosting" to create urgency.** If the other side believes negotiations are going well, then suddenly communication stops, they will often start negotiating against themselves, offering better terms just to get the conversation back on track.

- **Introducing unnecessary delays.** Pretending that a key decision-maker is unavailable, needing additional time for legal review, or introducing unexpected last-minute hurdles can exhaust the other side, making them more willing to accept suboptimal terms just to close the deal.

Real-World Example:
How Li Ka-Shing Used Silence and Delays to Secure a Billion-Dollar Property in Hong Kong

Li Ka-Shing, one of Asia's most powerful real estate investors, has long been known for his ability to manipulate timing and pressure in negotiations. One of his most effective tactics is using silence and delays to create uncertainty, forcing the other party into a weaker position.

In the early 2000s, Li was interested in acquiring a prime waterfront development site in Hong Kong. The seller, a struggling developer burdened with debt, was holding out for a high price, assuming Li would be eager to close quickly. But instead of negotiating aggressively, Li did something unexpected—he went completely silent.

For weeks, he ignored follow-ups, made no counteroffers, and let the seller sit in uncertainty. As time passed, the seller grew anxious, wondering if they had overplayed their hand. Meanwhile, their financial situation worsened, and their need for liquidity became urgent.

Just when the seller was at their breaking point, Li returned with an offer—one far lower than what they had originally asked for. By then, they had no choice but to accept, as the market had cooled, and no other buyers had come forward. Li secured the property at a steep discount, not by outbidding competitors, but by simply allowing time and silence to work in his favor.

This deal was a classic example of how delays and silence can turn a seller's confidence into desperation. When uncertainty builds, people start second-guessing themselves, often making concessions just to regain a sense of control. Li understood this psychological pressure better than anyone, using it to his advantage and walking away with an incredible deal.

This is why billionaires and elite entrepreneurs never appear rushed in negotiations. They create a sense of calm control, while the other side feels the pressure of time ticking away.

Controlling the pace of the negotiation allows a negotiator to make the other side feel like they are constantly reacting rather than leading. This shift in dynamics increases the chances of securing better terms with minimal resistance.

Winning the Deal Before the First Offer Is Made

Most people believe negotiations begin when the first offer is presented, but top dealmakers know that the real work happens long before that moment. The best deals are won before the negotiation even starts, simply by shaping the circumstances in a way that forces the other party to accept a predetermined outcome.

- **Positioning yourself as the only logical choice.** When they negotiate a deal, they don't enter a room as just another bidder or participant—they enter as the only viable option. This is done through branding, pre-negotiation discussions, and eliminating competitors behind the scenes.

- **Setting up conditions where the other side needs the deal.** If a company or investor feels like their survival, reputation, or success depends on closing the deal, they will compromise far more than they otherwise would. The best negotiators understand these psychological and financial pressures and use them to extract value.

- **Controlling the perception of the deal.** The party that frames the narrative has the upper hand. If the negotiation is positioned as an exclusive opportunity, a rescue deal, or a once-in-a-lifetime partnership, the other side is more likely to act with urgency and agree to terms they might otherwise resist.

Real-World Example:
How Samuel Liberman Secured Prime Land in São Paulo Before the First Offer Was Made

Samuel Liberman, one of Brazil's most influential real estate billionaires, built his fortune by acquiring high-value land in São Paulo before competitors even had a chance to bid. His approach was simple but ruthless: he never entered a deal as just another buyer—he ensured he was the only real option before the first offer was ever made.

One of his most masterful plays came when he secured a coveted development site in the heart of São Paulo's financial district, an area where top developers had been competing for years. The land was owned by a family trust, and while there was interest from multiple bidders, Liberman set the stage so that by the time negotiations officially started, the family had no other viable choice but to sell to him.

- **Positioning Himself as the Only Logical Buyer**

  Before approaching the family, Liberman worked behind the scenes to lock up all nearby properties and infrastructure approvals. By the time the family considered selling, he had already secured zoning changes and infrastructure support from the city government, making any competing bidder face a mountain of regulatory hurdles. If they sold to him, the deal would be quick and seamless. If they sold to anyone else, the process would be slow and uncertain.

- **Setting Up Conditions Where the Seller Needed Him**

  The family wasn't in a rush to sell, but Liberman knew that market cycles wouldn't wait forever. Through carefully placed media stories and industry speculation, he created the perception that development costs were about to rise significantly, subtly pushing the family into feeling like their best window to sell was closing fast.

- **Controlling the Perception of the Deal**

Instead of engaging in a traditional bidding war, Liberman arranged private meetings with the family, positioning himself not just as a buyer but as a long-term partner who would honor the family's legacy. He even structured the deal so that the family would retain a small ownership stake in the future development, giving them a reason to choose him over other potential buyers.

When the time came to make an offer, there was no competition left. The family accepted his terms, knowing that he had eliminated risk, secured approvals, and given them a financial upside beyond a simple sale.

By the time rival developers realized what had happened, Liberman had already closed the deal, secured the land, and controlled one of the most valuable real estate assets in São Paulo.

Lesson: The Best Dealmakers Don't Wait—They Control the Outcome Before Negotiations Even Begin

Samuel Liberman didn't enter a bidding war—he made sure there wasn't one. By securing approvals, removing alternatives, and shaping the narrative, he positioned himself as the only logical buyer. This is how billionaires operate—they don't fight for deals, they ensure the deal is already theirs before anyone else even has a chance to bid.

By structuring the deal before it even begins, top negotiators ensure they never enter a fair fight. The outcome is already in their favor before the first word is spoken

How Billionaires View Risk, Control, and Long-Term Strategy

The average person negotiates based on short-term results—saving money, winning concessions, or feeling like they "got a deal." Billionaires take a long-term view, structuring deals so they profit from them for years, not just at closing.

- **Risk is something to be transferred, not taken.** The most powerful negotiators ensure that others absorb the financial, operational, and legal risks while they extract profits with minimal exposure.

- **Control is more important than ownership.** They do not need to own 100% of an asset to dictate how it operates. They secure board seats, voting rights, and contractual advantages that allow them to control key decisions without taking on the full liability.

- **Future upside is always built into the deal.** Instead of making a one-time profit, they negotiate for revenue-sharing agreements, stock options, or liquidation preferences that ensure they benefit even after exiting the deal.

A well-negotiated deal should continue generating wealth long after the ink has dried. That's why top dealmakers never just focus on price—they focus on structuring the financial and operational terms to their advantage.

The Power of Walking Away and Making the Other Side Desperate

One of the strongest weapons in negotiation is the ability to walk away—but only when used strategically. Billionaire negotiators don't just threaten to leave a deal; they create situations where the other party cannot afford for them to walk away.

- **Desperation forces bad decisions.** When one side needs the deal more than the other, they will make concessions they would not have considered otherwise.

- **Alternatives provide power.** The reason top dealmakers can walk away is that they always have backup options—whether it's another buyer, a different investor, or a competing acquisition.

- **Time pressure works in their favor.** By delaying, stalling, or introducing obstacles, they increase stress on the other party, making them more likely to agree to terms they would otherwise reject.

Appearing desperate is one of the quickest ways to lose in a negotiation. The side that can afford to walk away almost always dictates the terms.

Lessons: Carl Icahn and Henry Kravis

The world's most successful negotiators don't try to win arguments—they structure the game so they cannot lose.

Carl Icahn's Strategy:
Turning Corporate Weakness Into Profit

Carl Icahn built his empire by targeting struggling companies, applying intense pressure on management, and extracting massive payouts without taking full ownership. Unlike traditional investors who focus on long-term growth, Icahn specialized in identifying companies in distress and forcing leadership to make decisions that prioritized his financial gain over the company's future.

Identifying Companies in Vulnerable Positions

- He focused on companies with excessive debt, poor leadership, or declining profitability. These businesses were often desperate for capital or a turnaround strategy, making them more susceptible to external pressure.

- He looked for shareholder dissatisfaction and weak governance. Companies where investors were unhappy with management provided an easy opportunity to rally support for major changes.

- He targeted businesses trading below their potential value. If a company was worth more in pieces than as a whole, he would push for asset sales or spin-offs to unlock value.

Gaining Influence Without Full Ownership

- He rarely sought majority control or full ownership. Instead, he acquired just enough shares—typically between 5% and 20%—to gain significant influence over corporate decisions.

- He used proxy fights to replace board members. By securing board seats, he could steer the company in a direction that benefited him financially.

- He forced leadership changes without taking operational responsibility. Icahn's goal was never to run the company but to install executives who would prioritize shareholder returns over long-term investments.

Using Public Pressure to Force Concessions

- He engaged in aggressive public criticism of management. By openly attacking CEOs and board members, he created pressure for leadership to adopt his demands.

- He leveraged media coverage to amplify his influence. When Icahn publicly declared his stake in a company, it often triggered stock price movements and increased pressure on executives to respond.

- He framed his actions as advocating for shareholders. By positioning himself as the champion of investor interests, he gained support from other shareholders and increased his negotiating power.

Extracting Maximum Payouts and Walking Away

- He pressured companies to buy back shares and issue special dividends. This strategy allowed him to quickly recover his investment and secure profits without relying on long-term business success.

- He forced asset sales and restructuring. If a company had valuable subsidiaries or underutilized assets, he pushed for sell-offs that increased stock prices in the short term.

- He exited as soon as he maximized his gains. Unlike traditional investors who stayed for sustained growth, Icahn sold his shares once he extracted the most value, often leaving companies weaker than before.

The Icahn Playbook: Profit Through Pressure

Icahn's approach was not about improving companies—it was about finding financial weaknesses, exploiting management failures, and securing fast, high-return paydays. His ability to force companies into desperate negotiations made him one of the most feared investors in corporate America

Henry Kravis
and the Power of Leveraged Buyouts

Henry Kravis transformed corporate finance by pioneering the aggressive use of leveraged buyouts (LBOs), a strategy that allowed him to acquire billion-dollar companies with minimal personal financial exposure. His method was simple but highly effective—use borrowed money to finance acquisitions, restructure the company for maximum short-term profitability, and exit with massive returns. This approach allowed him to gain control over major corporations while shifting the financial risk onto lenders and the companies themselves.

Using Borrowed Money to Buy Billion-Dollar Companies

- Kravis recognized that traditional acquisitions required massive capital investments, which limited the number of deals an investor could make. By using debt instead of his own money, he could acquire multiple companies at once, multiplying his returns.

- His firm, Kohlberg Kravis Roberts & Co. (KKR), pioneered a structure where the target company's own assets were used as collateral for loans. This meant the company, not Kravis or KKR, was responsible for repaying the debt.

- Because the deals were backed by the assets of the acquired companies, lenders were willing to finance huge buyouts, even for companies worth billions. This enabled Kravis to pursue deals that would have been impossible through traditional financing.

Minimizing Financial Risk While Maintaining Control

- Since Kravis and KKR were not personally guaranteeing the debt, their financial exposure was limited. If a company struggled to repay the loans, it was the lenders and existing shareholders who bore the losses—not Kravis or his firm.

- By securing board seats and appointing management teams aligned with KKR's interests, Kravis could dictate major corporate decisions without having to own a majority of the stock.

- Even in cases where a company failed after an LBO, KKR had often already extracted massive profits through special dividends, management fees, and asset sales, ensuring they still walked away with gains.

Restructuring Companies for Maximum Profitability

- Once KKR acquired a company, Kravis focused on aggressively cutting costs, selling non-core assets, and streamlining operations to boost short-term profitability.

- He often replaced existing management teams with executives who prioritized financial performance over long-term growth, making the company more attractive for resale.

- By rapidly increasing the company's value through cost-cutting and operational changes, KKR could sell the company at a premium within a few years, generating massive returns.

The Lasting Impact of Kravis's Strategy

- His landmark buyout of RJR Nabisco in 1988 for $31 billion was one of the most famous deals in financial history, proving that even massive corporations could be taken over through LBOs.

- The success of his deals cemented LBOs as a dominant force in private equity, influencing how buyouts and corporate takeovers are structured today.

- **His approach demonstrated that control, not ownership, was the key to financial power.** By using borrowed money and strategic influence, he built a financial empire without taking on the risks traditionally associated with massive corporate acquisitions.

Henry Kravis didn't just change how deals were done—he changed the entire landscape of corporate finance, proving that with the right structure, investors could acquire and control billion-dollar companies without risking their own fortunes

These dealmakers don't rely on luck or persuasion. They structure negotiations so that success is built into the agreement before it's even signed

CHAPTER 2:

The Illusion of Choice –
Controlling the Deal Before It Starts

Most people believe that negotiation starts when two parties sit down at the table. But elite dealmakers I have dealt with over my 35 years in doing this know that by the time an official negotiation begins, the outcome should already be set in motion. *They don't wait to debate terms—they engineer the entire situation beforehand,* making sure the other party is walking into a controlled environment where they have limited alternatives and little leverage.

This is the illusion of choice: making the other side believe they are making decisions while, in reality, every available option benefits the person who set the stage. When executed correctly, the other party feels like they are actively participating in shaping the deal, when in truth, they are simply choosing between different paths that all lead to the same destination.

How Elite Dealmakers
Engineer Negotiations Before They Even Begin

The best negotiators don't enter a room hoping for favorable terms, they design the playing field in advance. They remove the other side's alternatives, dictate the flow of information, and create an environment where the final decision is inevitable.

Limiting Choices Before the Deal Starts

Look, let's be honest; one of the most powerful ways to control a negotiation is to eliminate alternatives before discussions even begin. The more limited the other party's options, the stronger your position. By the time negotiations start, the other side should already feel like they have no better alternative.

- **Securing key partnerships in advance.** If a business relies on specific suppliers, distributors, or financial backers, an astute dealmaker can quietly establish exclusive agreements with those parties before making an offer. This ensures that the other side (competition) cannot seek competitive bids or find alternative support.

- **Controlling access to financing.** If the other party (competitor) requires funding, an experienced negotiator will secure commitments from key lenders or investors beforehand. This can make it difficult for the other side to seek independent financing, forcing them into the deal under pre-set terms.

- **Eliminating competing buyers or investors.** If the goal is to acquire a company, a savvy dealmaker might privately approach competitors and offer them separate opportunities, ensuring they opt out of the bidding process. In real estate, this could mean securing zoning approvals or strategic partnerships that make it impossible for others to compete for the same asset.

By taking these steps before making an offer, a negotiator removes potential escape routes, leaving the other party feeling boxed in. When executed correctly, the other side walks into negotiations already believing that their only viable option is the deal on the table.

Shaping the Perception of Value

People don't make decisions based on absolute value—they make them based on **perceived** value. A skilled negotiator ensures that the other party believes they are getting the best possible deal, even if they are actually walking into a well-structured trap.

- **Creating a sense of exclusivity.** If an opportunity feels scarce, it becomes more valuable. By limiting access to a deal—whether by saying there are "only a few spots left" or making it an "invite-only opportunity"—negotiators increase the perceived value of what they are offering. But this needs to be done tactfully, tastefully and professionally. Meaning not "salesy".

- **Using false urgency.** Deadlines, expiring offers, and competitive pressure force people to act quickly. When buyers or investors believe they only have a short window to decide, they are less likely to conduct due diligence or explore alternatives. We saw this immensely a few years back in the residential real estate market! Buyers were bidding FULL value, site unseen, no inspection. Sellers had the upper hand and they used it.

- **Selective information release.** Instead of revealing everything upfront, dealmakers strategically control what information is made available. By emphasizing strong aspects of the deal and downplaying potential risks, they can shape how the other party perceives the opportunity.

The key is to ensure that the other side **feels like they are winning**, even when the deal is structured to overwhelmingly benefit the strategist. When someone believes they have found the best possible deal, they stop looking for alternatives, allowing the dealmaker to maintain control.

Controlling Timing and External Pressure

The best negotiators understand that time is not just a factor—it is a weapon. When the other party feels rushed, uncertain, or under pressure, they become far more likely to accept unfavorable terms just to reach a resolution.

- **Manipulating deadlines.** Imposing artificial deadlines forces the other side to act before they are fully prepared. Statements like "This offer is only valid until the end of the week" or "We have another buyer ready to sign" create a psychological urgency that speeds up decision-making.

- **Using external pressures to create fear.** If a company is facing a financial deadline, an experienced dealmaker will delay discussions until the pressure is at its peak. When people are backed into a corner, they are willing to accept terms they normally wouldn't consider.

- **Introducing last-minute obstacles.** Just when the other side believes they have secured a fair deal, a negotiator might introduce new terms, unexpected delays, or legal reviews that stretch out the process. This can wear down the other party, making them more likely to accept unfavorable adjustments just to close the deal.

By ensuring that the other side feels pressed for time and short on options, a skilled negotiator can secure better terms while making the other party feel like they reached the best decision on their own.

Using Pre-Negotiation Tactics
to Remove Alternative Options

One of the most effective ways to control a negotiation is to ensure the other side has nowhere else to turn. If they feel like they are walking into a conversation with multiple options, they will negotiate aggressively. But if they feel like they have no other viable choices, they will be forced to work within the constraints set for them.

- **Blocking alternative buyers, partners, or financiers.** The best dealmakers quietly secure exclusivity agreements, tie up potential investors, or influence key decision-makers before negotiations even begin.

- **Leveraging relationships to apply pressure.** If competitors, suppliers, or financiers are already aligned with the dealmaker, the other party quickly realizes that their alternatives have disappeared.

- **Controlling liquidity and financing options.** If a company needs funding but finds that every reasonable financing source is either unavailable or aligned with the buyer, they have little choice but to accept the terms on the table.

Real-World Example: How Sam Zell Eliminated Alternatives to Acquire the Chicago Tribune

Sam Zell (The Grave Dancer!!!!), one of the most legendary real estate investors and dealmakers, is a master at structuring negotiations where the other side has no choice but to accept his terms. One of his boldest moves came when he orchestrated the acquisition of the Chicago Tribune in 2007.

- Before Zell even entered formal negotiations, he systematically removed alternative buyers. The Tribune Company was struggling, and several potential investors had been circling. Zell quietly leveraged his connections in finance and media to create doubt among competitors, discouraging them from making serious offers.

- Knowing that the Tribune Company needed liquidity but had limited financing options, he secured commitments from major lenders before stepping into the negotiation room. When Tribune executives explored other funding sources, they found that most banks and investors had already been aligned with Zell's vision or saw him as the inevitable buyer.

- He also built internal support within the company. By the time negotiations officially began, key decision-makers within Tribune were already leaning toward Zell as the best (and only) viable option, giving him leverage to dictate favorable terms.

With no competitive bids, no alternative financing sources, and no internal opposition, Zell structured the deal entirely on his terms, acquiring the company with minimal risk. Tribune had nowhere else to turn, and Zell walked away controlling one of the most influential media companies in America.

This is how elite dealmakers win before the negotiation even starts—by making sure the other side has no escape routes left.

By ensuring that every escape route is closed off before the deal starts, elite negotiators make it nearly impossible for the other side to push back.

How to Make the Other Side Feel Like They Are Making Choices— While You Control Every Outcome

The best negotiators don't force terms onto the other side outright. Instead, they present multiple options, each leading to a controlled outcome. This keeps the other party engaged in the process and prevents them from realizing they are being led.

Offering Structured Choices Instead of Demands

One of the most effective ways to control a negotiation that I have found without making the other party feel pressured is to present structured choices rather than issuing direct demands. Instead of framing the conversation as "take it or leave it," a skilled negotiator guides the other party toward an outcome by giving them multiple paths—all of which lead to the same destination.

This technique works because people resist being forced into a single decision, but they feel empowered when they believe they have options. By offering two or more alternatives, a negotiator creates the illusion of choice while ensuring that every option benefits them.

How It Works in Practice

- In a business acquisition: Instead of telling a seller, "I'm offering $10 million for your company," a negotiator might say, "Would you prefer $8 million upfront with a performance-based bonus or $10 million over three years with a structured payout?" Either way, the buyer dictates the financial terms, but the seller feels like they are choosing the one that works best for them.

- In a real estate deal: A developer negotiating with a city for zoning approvals might say, "Would you prefer that we build a mixed-use property with a community park contribution, or would you rather have a commercial space with additional retail tax revenue?" Both options lead to the developer getting what they want, but the city feels like they are actively participating in the decision.

- In a salary negotiation: An employer might say, "Would you prefer a higher base salary with a smaller bonus structure or a lower base salary with uncapped commission potential?" This way, the company controls the financial exposure, but the candidate believes they are customizing their compensation package.

Framing Concessions as Victories

A skilled negotiator understands that people want to feel like they've won something in a deal. Even if they don't get everything they initially wanted, walking away with a perceived victory lowers resistance and makes them more likely to accept the overall terms. This is why elite dealmakers strategically offer small, calculated concessions—not because they have to, but because it makes the other party more cooperative while ensuring the bigger picture remains unchanged.

How to Frame Concessions as Wins

- **Offering something of low cost but high perceived value.** If a real estate investor is negotiating the purchase of a property, they might allow the seller to keep a small storage unit or parking space on-site. This doesn't impact the overall deal but makes the seller feel like they negotiated a better outcome.

- **Compromising on a minor point to protect the main objective.** If a private equity firm is buying a company and negotiating employment contracts with the executives, they might agree to a slightly higher salary for a key leader—but only in exchange for stricter performance metrics. The executive feels like they won a battle, but the firm maintains control over financial risk.

- **Timing the concession for maximum psychological impact.** Concessions should be made at **the right moment**—ideally, when the other party is starting to show hesitation. If they feel like they have fought for a small victory, they are less likely to push hard on bigger issues.

Real-World Example:
How Blackstone Used a Small Concession to Secure a Billion-Dollar Real Estate Deal

When Blackstone was negotiating the acquisition of a massive office portfolio from a struggling real estate firm, they knew the seller was emotionally attached to the properties but also financially pressured to sell. Instead of pushing hard and risking resistance, Blackstone strategically framed a minor concession as a victory to make the seller feel like they were getting a better deal.

- The seller initially wanted to retain one of the buildings in the portfolio, but Blackstone had no interest in breaking up the package. Rather than rejecting the request outright, *they countered with a different, low-cost concession—allowing the seller to keep naming rights on one of the flagship properties for five years.*

- This simple concession had no financial impact on Blackstone but gave the seller a public and emotional win, making them feel like they had fought for and secured something meaningful.

- **The psychological effect was immediate**. Feeling like they had won a key battle, the seller became far more cooperative on the final deal terms. Meanwhile, Blackstone kept control over what really mattered—the full acquisition of the portfolio on their terms.

In the end, Blackstone walked away with the entire real estate portfolio intact, while the seller got to save face and feel like they had negotiated a better outcome.

This is how the world's top dealmakers operate—they give up something that seems significant but costs them nothing to keep full control over the bigger picture. By strategically framing minor compromises as big wins for the other party, negotiators make the other side more invested in the deal while keeping the core structure of the agreement intact.

Creating Artificial Urgency

Time pressure is one of the most effective tools in dealmaking. The moment someone believes that an opportunity is slipping away, they become more willing to commit—often without fully analyzing whether they are getting the best deal. Elite negotiators know how to create a sense of urgency that forces the other party to act quickly, limiting their ability to rethink, shop around, or demand better terms.

How to Manufacture Urgency in Negotiations

- **Setting false deadlines.** Even if there is no actual rush, saying things like, "This offer is only good until Friday," forces the other party to make a decision quickly, before they have time to explore other options.

- **Introducing competitive pressure.** Savvy negotiators understand that perception drives urgency. Creating the illusion of scarcity and competition forces the opposing party to act decisively, often on less favorable terms. Rather than appearing overly eager, strategic ambiguity about competing offers shifts leverage in your favor.

- **A well-placed statement such as,** *"I have another serious buyer prepared to proceed, but I wanted to extend you the first opportunity,"* subtly alters the power dynamic. Whether or not a competing bidder exists is secondary—the goal is to manufacture decision pressure by introducing the risk of loss.

- **This tactic capitalizes on FOMO** (fear of missing out), anchoring bias, and loss aversion, psychological triggers that drive decision-makers to commit faster, negotiate less aggressively, and accept terms they might otherwise challenge. Advanced negotiators refine this by:

- **Varying the level of competitive pressure.** Too much urgency raises suspicion; too little fails to create action.

- **Embedding competition subtly.** Referencing market interest indirectly ("We're seeing strong activity in this space") often works better than blatant threats.

- **Timing competitive signals.** Introducing a competing offer at a strategic moment—right before closing—can push hesitant parties over the edge.

- The key is controlling the narrative. A well-executed competitive bluff, even without an actual rival, **forces the other side to negotiate against a phantom opponent—one they can't analyze, delay, or outmaneuver**

- **Using external factors as justification.** Instead of creating urgency out of thin air, an experienced negotiator will tie it to outside market conditions: "Interest rates are about to go up, and this pricing won't be available after next week," or "Our funding partners need to finalize commitments by Monday." This makes it seem like the timeline is dictated by external forces rather than a pressure tactic.

Why Artificial Urgency Works

- **It forces quick decisions.** The less time someone has to analyze a deal, the more likely they are to commit based on emotion rather than logic.

- **It reduces negotiation friction.** When people feel like they must act fast, they tend to negotiate less aggressively, fearing they might lose the opportunity altogether.

- **It prevents them from exploring alternatives.** Someone who believes they only have one shot at a deal won't waste time looking for other options—they will focus on securing what's in front of them.

By making the other side feel like they are working against the clock, dealmakers keep control of the negotiation process while ensuring a faster, smoother closing without unnecessary resistance.Top of FormBottom of Form

Real-World Case Study: How Sam Zell Engineered the Sale of Equity Office Properties for $39 Billion

Sam Zell's 2007 sale of Equity Office Properties (EOP) to Blackstone Group was a masterclass in negotiation strategy. He didn't just sell at the peak of the market—he controlled every element of the process, ensuring that buyers felt they were in control while he dictated the terms.

At first glance, it seemed like Zell was simply capitalizing on demand in commercial real estate. In reality, he had been setting up the deal long before any official offers were made. By structuring the process carefully, he forced buyers into a competitive bidding war, maximizing his exit price while minimizing his risks.

How Zell Positioned EOP for Maximum Leverage

Long before the sale was announced, Zell made sure that when the time came to negotiate, he would have all the leverage.

- **He built EOP into the largest publicly traded office landlord in the U.S.**, owning over 590 buildings and 105 million square feet of space. Any buyer looking to dominate the office market had to go through him.

- **He had already tested market interest quietly,** speaking with major investment firms before making the sale public. This created the perception that a rare opportunity was about to become available.

- **He structured the deal to be seen as a must-win for buyers like Blackstone.** By positioning EOP as a once-in-a-lifetime acquisition, he made firms feel they had to compete aggressively for the asset.

By the time EOP was officially put up for sale, the competition was already intense. Zell had engineered a situation where buyers were bidding against each other, not him.

Creating the Illusion of Choice for Buyers

The real genius of this deal wasn't just attracting buyers—it was making them feel like they had control over the process, even though Zell was the one dictating the terms.

- He allowed multiple bidders into the process but structured it so that Blackstone would feel pressure to move quickly. After Blackstone submitted an offer, he encouraged Vornado Realty Trust to enter the game, driving up the price.

- He made buyers choose between different deal structures, knowing both would ultimately benefit him. Vornado offered a higher price but wanted to pay in stock, while Blackstone preferred an all-cash deal. Zell made it seem like he was weighing both options carefully, forcing Blackstone to increase its bid.

- He controlled the pace of negotiations, using strategic delays to increase urgency. Blackstone feared losing the deal and raised its offer multiple times, eventually agreeing to a staggering $39 billion price tag.

What looked like a competitive bidding war was actually a carefully orchestrated strategy where Zell controlled every outcome.

The Outcome: Zell's Perfectly Timed Exit

He sold EOP at the absolute peak of the real estate market, just months before the 2008 financial crisis.

He personally walked away with over $1 billion from the sale.

Blackstone, despite "winning" the bidding war, was left holding billions in office real estate just as the market crashed.

The Takeaway

Zell's approach to this deal was a textbook example of how to control negotiations before they even start.

- He created a situation where buyers felt they were making decisions, when in reality, he had structured the entire process to benefit himself.

- He used competition, timing, and perceived scarcity to force buyers to act aggressively.

- He walked away with maximum profit, while the buyer assumed all the long-term risk.

What looked like a great victory for Blackstone was actually a **masterful negotiation strategy where Sam Zell had already won before the deal was even signed.**

CHAPTER 3:

Control Without Ownership –
The Real Key to Wealth

A lot of entrepreneurs believe that wealth comes from owning valuable assets, but the world's most powerful dealmakers know a deeper truth: control matters more than possession. Billionaires, hedge fund moguls, and private equity firms have mastered the art of structuring deals that give them power over assets without exposing themselves to unnecessary risk.

They use influence, leverage, and financial engineering to dictate terms, extract profit, and walk away without the burdens of direct ownership. This chapter breaks down how they do it— and how you can apply the same principles in your own deals.

The Myth of Ownership

Ownership is often an illusion. People assume that whoever holds the title to a business or property is the one in charge, but in reality, the real power lies in who controls the cash flow, decision-making, and exit strategy. The wealthiest investors don't seek ownership for its own sake; they seek control mechanisms that allow them to influence or dominate an asset without tying up their own money.

For example, Warren Buffett often structures deals that give him preferred shares, board seats, and influence over key decisions without taking full ownership. Carl Icahn and other activist investors buy minority stakes in companies and use voting rights, legal pressure, and financial tactics to force changes that benefit them. The result? They reap massive profits while someone else holds the long-term risk.

How the Smartest Investors
Control Assets Without Risking Their Own Money

Major firms like Blackstone, Apollo Global, and Carl Icahn Enterprises have perfected the art of acquiring power over assets without taking on the liabilities of ownership. They use strategic deal structures to:

- Gain **voting rights and board influence** to dictate corporate decisions

- Leverage **debt and investor capital** to acquire control while minimizing personal risk

- Set up **financial agreements that force companies to depend on them**

- Extract massive value from businesses while avoiding long-term exposure

For example, private equity firms like Apollo buy companies using mostly borrowed money, install their own management teams, and extract profits through fees and dividends—often before the company even turns a profit. If the business later struggles, they walk away without personal financial damage because the debt is in the company's name, not theirs.

Structuring Deals for Maximum Influence

Control is about setting the terms before anyone realizes the game has started. The most effective dealmakers use these methods to secure power without ownership:

- **Voting Rights & Board Seats:** A small percentage of shares can grant influence over company decisions.

- **Convertible Debt & Preferred Shares:** These give financial upside and influence while avoiding risk.

- **Leveraged Buyouts (LBOs):** Acquiring companies using borrowed money, ensuring personal funds are protected.

- **Proxy Battles & Shareholder Activism:** Forcing management to comply with their demands.

- **Joint Ventures & Master Lease Agreements:** Gaining Operational Control Without Ownership

Let's talk more on Master Leases as a tactic to gain control without ownership.

One of the most powerful strategies used by elite investors is acquiring control over real estate and businesses without actually buying them outright. Instead of tying up large amounts of capital, they leverage joint ventures and master lease agreements to operate, improve, and profit from assets while keeping their financial exposure minimal.

A master lease agreement (MLA) allows an investor to lease an entire property from the owner, take full operational control, and generate income from it as if they were the owner—without having to purchase it outright. This strategy is frequently used in distressed or underperforming assets where the property owner is struggling but unwilling (or unable) to sell. I also wrote the book on Master Leases as an acquisition tool. Check it out (www.MillionDollarMasterLeases.com)

How Blackstone Uses
Master Lease Agreements to Control Billions in Real Estate

One of the best real-world examples of this strategy is Blackstone, the world's largest private equity real estate firm. Instead of outright purchasing every asset they want to control, Blackstone often enters into master lease agreements with property owners, especially in sectors like hospitality, senior living, and office real estate.

- In hotel and senior living acquisitions, Blackstone has structured master lease deals where they take full control of operations, reposition the asset, and drive profitability—all while avoiding the upfront capital cost of buying the property.

- This approach allows them to maximize cash flow, enhance the asset's value, and eventually structure an exit on their terms, whether by flipping the lease to another investor, acquiring the property later at a favorable price, or taking it public as part of a larger portfolio.

- By using master leases, Blackstone shifts financial risk away from themselves while still reaping the benefits of ownership, such as tax advantages, revenue participation, and market control.

Why This Matters for Negotiators and Investors

Using joint ventures and master lease agreements is an advanced play that allows investors to control high-value assets with little to no money down. This strategy is particularly effective in markets where sellers are hesitant to sell but need a financial or operational partner to improve the asset.

For any investor looking to scale quickly without taking on excessive financial risk, this tactic can be a game-changer—allowing them to gain control, create value, and structure profitable exits without ever owning the property outright.

Case Study: How John Henry Controlled the Boston Red Sox Without Full Ownership

John Henry, the billionaire investor and founder of Fenway Sports Group, is a master of controlling valuable assets without fully owning them. His acquisition and management of the Boston Red Sox, as well as his expansion into global sports and media, demonstrate how **strategic influence, financial structuring, and leveraging partnerships** can yield maximum control while minimizing risk.

Rather than simply purchasing teams or businesses out-right with his own capital, Henry consistently **structures deals that give him authority and decision-making power** without overextending himself financially. His approach allows him to shape the future of his investments, extract significant profits, and expand his empire—all without taking on the full burden of ownership.

Acquiring the Red Sox
Without Overextending Himself

In 2001, the Boston Red Sox, one of Major League Baseball's most iconic franchises, went up for sale. Several deep-pocketed bidders, including cable TV mogul Charles Dolan, were in the mix. Unlike other bidders who aimed for outright ownership, Henry orchestrated a deal that spread the financial risk among multiple investors while ensuring he retained operational control.

- **Assembling a Strategic Investment Group**
  Instead of buying the Red Sox alone, Henry put together an investment group called New England Sports Ventures (NESV), now known as Fenway Sports Group (FSG). This group included key figures such as Tom Werner and The New York Times Company, allowing Henry to secure the necessary capital without shouldering the entire financial risk. By pooling resources, the group was able to acquire the team for $660 million while ensuring that Henry remained the primary decision-maker.

- **Negotiating for Maximum Control Despite Shared Ownership**
  Even though multiple investors contributed to the acquisition, Henry structured the deal in a way that gave him effective control over the team's operations, strategy, and key financial decisions. The voting rights and governance structure ensured that while other investors had a stake, they did not have equal influence over the direction of the franchise. This

allowed Henry to operate as if he were the sole owner, even though he did not personally finance the entire deal.

- **Leveraging Fenway Park as a Business Asset Without Full Ownership**
  Rather than simply purchasing Fenway Park outright, Henry capitalized on its value through strategic development rights, sponsorship deals, and premium revenue opportunities. By securing long-term partnerships and investing in renovations, he increased the stadium's profitability and modernized its infrastructure while minimizing financial exposure.

Henry's ability to structure deals where he controlled key assets without fully owning them was a game-changer in professional sports and set the stage for future acquisitions.

Expanding Influence Beyond the Red Sox Without Heavy Capital Investment

After securing control of the Red Sox, Henry used similar strategies to expand into **global sports, media, and entertainment** while maintaining financial flexibility.

- **Acquiring Liverpool FC with Minimal Personal Risk**
  In 2010, Henry and Fenway Sports Group purchased Liverpool Football Club for $343 million, a deal that mirrored his Red Sox acquisition. Instead of personally funding the entire purchase, he structured the transaction to rely on smart financing, debt restructuring, and strategic reinvestment in the club. Liverpool's financial struggles at the time made it an undervalued asset, allowing Henry to take over at a fraction of its future worth. Under his leadership, Liverpool's valuation **soared to over $4 billion**, proving the effectiveness of his approach.

- **Using Strategic Ownership Stakes to Expand Without Full Commitment**
  Henry did not stop with baseball and soccer. Through Fenway Sports Group, he expanded into other professional sports, acquiring the Pittsburgh Penguins in the NHL, Roush Fenway Keselowski Racing in NASCAR, and a major stake in the

regional sports media industry. In each case, rather than buying these entities outright, Henry structured deals that allowed him to control operations and strategy while other investors shared financial responsibility.

- **Acquiring the Boston Globe Without Full Integration into His Empire**
  In 2013, Henry purchased The Boston Globe for $70 million, but rather than folding it into Fenway Sports Group, he kept it separate as a privately held asset, allowing him to maintain control without it affecting his sports business empire. This strategic separation ensured that each of his investments remained financially insulated from the others, reducing overall risk.

Why Control Matters More Than Ownership

John Henry's business model is built on the idea that having decision-making authority is more valuable than outright ownership. By structuring deals that prioritize control, he ensures that he remains the primary power behind his investments while minimizing his financial exposure.

- He did not need to fully own the Red Sox to make every major decision affecting the team.

- He did not need to personally fund Liverpool's entire acquisition to turn it into a multibillion-dollar asset.

- He did not need to outright own the Boston Globe to influence the city's media landscape.

By consistently structuring deals that give him the power to lead without the burden of full financial responsibility, Henry has built one of the most successful sports and business empires in the world. His strategy proves that in high-stakes business, control is more valuable than possession, and influence is the real currency of power.

Kevin O'Leary's Ruthless Negotiation for Honeyfund – The No-Risk Equity Play

Kevin O'Leary, known as "Mr. Wonderful" on *Shark Tank*, has built his brand on one ruthless principle: Always structure deals where you win no matter what. He doesn't just negotiate equity stakes—he engineers financial leverage that ensures he gets paid first, minimizes risk, and locks in long-term profits whether the company succeeds or fails.

One of the best examples of this strategy in action was his investment in Honeyfund, a wedding registry company that allowed couples to crowdfund their honeymoon expenses instead of receiving traditional gifts. O'Leary's negotiation of this deal is a masterclass in structuring a no-risk, high-reward investment—and a brutal lesson for any entrepreneur who thinks they can out-negotiate a billionaire.

The Setup – A High-Value Business with a Major Weakness

When the Honeyfund founders walked into the *Shark Tank*, they had something every investor loves—a proven business model with millions in transactions already under their belt.

- **They had market traction** — Over $200 million in wedding gifts had already been processed through their platform.

- **They had a strong customer base** — Couples were actively using their service to fund honeymoons, meaning there was already demand.

- **They had momentum** — Unlike many startups pitching in the tank, Honeyfund wasn't just an idea—it was a revenue-generating business.

But there was a problem—and Mr. Wonderful spotted it immediately.

- **Revenue Model Weakness** — Honeyfund wasn't charging users directly. Instead, they were making money through affiliate deals and transaction partnerships. This meant they weren't fully monetizing the massive volume of money flowing through their platform.

- **Scaling Challenges** — The company had a solid foundation, but its path to explosive profitability was unclear. Without a clear strategy to increase revenue per user, long-term growth could be limited.

The founders were looking for an investor who could help them restructure their business model and take it to the next level—but what they didn't realize was that O'Leary had a completely different agenda.

Mr. Wonderful's Power Move —
The No-Risk Royalty Deal

Kevin O'Leary's Honeyfund Deal –
A Masterclass in Ruthless Negotiation

Kevin O'Leary, known as *Mr. Wonderful* on *Shark Tank,* has a reputation for cold-blooded, billionaire-style dealmaking—and his negotiation with Honeyfund was a textbook example of how elite investors eliminate risk while guaranteeing long-term profits.

When the Honeyfund founders entered the tank, they were looking for $400,000 in exchange for 10% equity, valuing their company at $4 million. Most investors would have immediately argued over valuation or asked for a bigger stake. They might have tried to drive down the valuation, take a larger percentage of ownership, or negotiate for control over operations.

O'Leary didn't do any of that. Instead of fighting over the standard investment terms, he restructured the deal entirely in a way that made sure he got paid immediately and indefinitely—whether the business succeeded or not.

This is the kind of power move that separates billionaire deal-makers from average investors. Let's break it down.

1. Shifting the Conversation from Equity to Guaranteed Returns

Most investors on *Shark Tank* operate within the typical equity-based investment model—they provide capital in exchange for a percentage of the company, then hope the company grows and becomes valuable over time. This is risky because:

- If the company fails, the investor loses everything.

- If the company struggles, the investor is stuck holding equity that may never turn into real cash.

- The investor only gets paid when there's a liquidity event (such as selling the company or an IPO), which could take years or never happen at all.

O'Leary refused to play this game. Instead of negotiating based on future potential, he forced the deal into a structure where he would get paid immediately—from every single transaction the company made.

His strategy was brilliant:

- Instead of just owning 10% of the company, he wanted a royalty on every single dollar that passed through the platform.

- This meant that whether the company was profitable or not, whether it scaled or not, whether it was sold or not—O'Leary would still make money.

Why this is a power move:

- With traditional equity, investors only make money if the company does well.

- With a royalty structure, O'Leary made money whether the company did well or not.

- He shifted the entire risk burden onto the founders while ensuring a steady stream of cash flow for himself.

2. Structuring the Deal So He Got Paid First

Now that he had set up the royalty model, O'Leary took it one step further—he made sure that his money came out first, before anyone else got paid.

Here's how he structured it:

- He agreed to invest $400,000, but only under the following conditions:

  ▷ He would receive $1 per transaction until he recouped his entire $400,000 investment.

  ▷ Once his investment was fully paid back, the royalty would drop to $0.50 per transaction—but it would never go away.

This completely changed the game.

- Instead of waiting years to see a return, O'Leary was getting paid back immediately from every customer transaction.

- The founders had to keep working just to pay him back—they carried all the risk, while he sat back and collected money.

- And once his investment was repaid, he still had a permanent revenue stream from every future transaction.

The Genius of This Structure

- He recovered his investment first, before anyone else made a profit.

  ▷ This ensured he would never lose money, no matter what happened.

- He created a long-term royalty stream, guaranteeing a passive income.

  ▷ Even after the company paid him back, they still had to keep paying him indefinitely.

- He turned a one-time investment into a permanent money machine.

  ▷ Most investors hope for a return in years. O'Leary set up a system where he would start making money from day one.

3. Minimizing Risk While Maximizing Upside

At this point, O'Leary had already removed all risk from the deal, but he wasn't done yet. He still took the 10% equity stake, which gave him long-term upside in case the business became a massive success.

Here's how this played out:

- If Honeyfund became a billion-dollar company, O'Leary would still own 10% of that future value—a massive potential return.

- But if the business struggled or failed, it wouldn't matter—because he had already taken his money back through the royalties.

Why This Strategy Is So Powerful

- If the company does well, O'Leary wins big.

- If the company does okay, O'Leary still wins.

- If the company fails, O'Leary still gets paid back first and walks away without a loss.

This is the ultimate negotiation power move—setting up a deal where you make money in every possible scenario.

The Takeaway:
The Ultimate Cold-Blooded Negotiation Strategy

Kevin O'Leary's Honeyfund deal is a perfect example of how elite billionaires structure deals to eliminate risk and ensure profits.

Most investors play the game hoping to win. O'Leary plays the game so he can't lose.

Key Lessons for High-Stakes Negotiation:

- **Control the cash flow.**

  ▷ Instead of waiting on future profits, get paid upfront and ensure money flows to you before anyone else.

- **Recover your investment first.**

  ▷ If you're putting money into a deal, structure it so you get paid back as fast as possible.

- **Set up long-term passive income.**

  ▷ A smart deal isn't just about making money once—it's about securing a continuous cash flow.

- **Minimize your risk, maximize your upside.**

  ▷ Always structure deals so you win in every possible scenario—whether the business succeeds, struggles, or fails.

- **Make your money independent of the company's success.**

  ▷ Don't just rely on equity. Find ways to make money even if the business doesn't scale

This deal structure was brilliantly ruthless—Honeyfund still gave up 10% equity, but more importantly, they gave up a percentage of every future transaction indefinitely.

The Psychological Squeeze —
How Mr. Wonderful Forced the Deal

The Honeyfund founders hesitated when O'Leary first made his offer. They knew the royalty would cost them far more over time than just giving up more equity.

But O'Leary knew exactly how to pressure them into saying yes:

- **Credibility & Authority** – He positioned himself as the smartest financial mind in the room, making it clear that other Sharks didn't understand how to structure a deal like this. By presenting himself as the best option for long-term financial success, he created doubt in the founders' minds about rejecting his offer.

- **Scarcity & Urgency** – He threatened to walk away, making it clear that this was their one shot at getting a deal with him. He played on their fear of missing out, forcing them to make a decision under pressure.

- **Reframing the Deal as a Win** – O'Leary spun the royalty structure as a positive, claiming it would help them scale without giving up too much equity. He made them feel like they were keeping control of their company—when in reality, they were giving him a permanent revenue stream.

Feeling the pressure, the founders accepted the deal—and in doing so, they locked themselves into one of the most one-sided deals in Shark Tank history.

The Outcome —
Why Mr. Wonderful Won (Again)

By structuring the deal as a royalty-based investment instead of straight equity, O'Leary guaranteed himself a cash flow machine:

- He got paid first—before the founders, before other investors, and before the company made any profit.

- He reduced his risk to nearly zero, since he was recouping his capital before anything else.

- He locked in a long-term, guaranteed revenue stream that would scale as the business grew.

This was classic Cold-Blooded Billionaire Negotiation Tactics—O'Leary manipulated the deal structure, ensured he got paid upfront, and created a scenario where he won, no matter what happened to the business.

Key Lessons from Mr. Wonderful's Ruthless Deal

This negotiation isn't just a Shark Tank success story—it's a textbook lesson in structuring a negotiation where you control every possible outcome.

1. **Always Negotiate for Guaranteed Returns Before Equity**
   Most investors fight over equity percentages—but the real money is in controlling the cash flow. O'Leary structured the deal so that he got paid before the founders did, meaning he was in a risk-free position.

2. **Make Sure You Get Paid First**
   If you're negotiating any deal, make sure your money comes out before anyone else gets their cut. Whether it's royalties, dividends, or preferential payouts, ensure you're not waiting to make money while others profit first.

3. **Use Urgency & Scarcity to Force Concessions**
   O'Leary didn't wait for Honeyfund to make up their minds—he created urgency, pressuring them to make a decision on his terms. The best negotiators understand that if the other side feels time pressure, they're more likely to give in.

4. **Reframe the Deal to Make It Feel Like a Win**
   Even though Honeyfund was losing money in the long run, O'Leary made it seem like they were getting a great deal. By shifting the focus to "scaling without losing too much equity," he convinced them to hand over perpetual revenue without even realizing what they gave up

CHAPTER 4

Information Asymmetry —
Winning Before the
Other Side Knows the Game

The best negotiators don't approach deals on equal footing, they ensure that they have more information than the other party, allowing them to dictate terms without resistance. This strategy is called **information asymmetry**—where one side holds a critical advantage simply by knowing more, while the other side makes decisions based on incomplete or misleading data.

Amateur negotiators strive for "fair" discussions, but elite dealmakers **exploit knowledge gaps** to create leverage, structure deals in their favor, and secure massive profits before their counterpart even realizes they've been outmaneuvered.

Why Information Asymmetry Works

- The less the other side knows, the fewer options they see.

- Controlling the flow of information allows you to shape perceptions of value.

- Deliberate misinformation can make competitors overpay or undervalue their own assets.

- When you know the real market conditions and the other side doesn't, you can dictate the terms of the deal.

- People negotiate based on the information they have—if you control that information, you control their decision-making.

Real World Example:
The Texan Oil Deal That Made Millions

Information asymmetry is the ultimate power play in high-stakes deals. When one side knows significantly more than the other, they control the narrative, the valuation, and the outcome. The best negotiators don't just react to deals—they shape them by controlling the flow of critical information.

A perfect example of this strategy in action is a classic Texan oil deal in 1983 where a savvy investor leveraged hidden market conditions, misinformation, and controlled data to walk away with millions—while the other side never knew what hit them.

How Information Asymmetry Gives You the Edge

- **The Less the Other Side Knows, the Fewer Options They See**

  In any deal, the side with the least information is at a massive disadvantage. If a landowner believes their oil-rich land is just an average property with minimal reserves, they'll be happy to sell at a discount. The buyer, armed with geological surveys and insider knowledge, can quietly scoop up the asset for pennies on the dollar.

- **Controlling the Flow of Information Allows You to Shape Perceptions of Value**

  In 1983, a Texas oil tycoon learned that a struggling rancher was sitting on a vast but untapped oil reserve. The rancher had been approached by other buyers but had been told by local geologists that the land was only "moderately valuable." The oil tycoon, having privately consulted top petroleum engineers, knew the truth—there were millions of barrels of oil beneath that land. Instead of revealing this, he downplayed the potential, agreeing with the rancher's assumption that the land wasn't worth much beyond cattle grazing.

- **Deliberate Misinformation Can Make Competitors Overpay or Undervalue Their Own Assets**

Before making his offer, the tycoon spread a false narrative through industry contacts, hinting that the area was experiencing rapid depletion of oil reserves—making it seem like drilling was becoming unprofitable. Competitors, hearing this, began pulling back from the region, assuming the land wasn't worth bidding on. This left the rancher with fewer buyers and lower offers, while the Fort Worth oil baron positioned himself as the "only real option" willing to pay cash.

- **When You Know the Real Market Conditions and the Other Side Doesn't, You Can Dictate the Terms of the Deal**
Armed with superior knowledge, the tycoon made an all-cash offer well below market value. The rancher, unaware of the true worth of his land, accepted, thinking he was getting a fair deal. Within six months, the tycoon sold drilling rights to a major oil company, walking away with 10 times his initial investment before a single barrel was even extracted.

- **People Negotiate Based on the Information They Have—If You Control That Information, You Control Their Decision-Making**
The key to this strategy was not just knowing more—but ensuring that no one else knew what he knew. By controlling the narrative, spreading doubt, and playing the role of a "modest buyer," the tycoon engineered a deal where he won before the other side even realized what was happening.

The Takeaway

In negotiation, knowledge isn't just power—it's profit. Whether you're buying oil fields, real estate, or businesses, the person who controls the flow of information dictates the deal. In the Texan oil deal, one man turned a struggling ranch into an oil fortune simply by knowing more—and making sure the other side knew less

Tactics for Using Information Asymmetry

Controlling Data Flow

Elite negotiators ensure that the other party never has a full picture of the deal. By carefully managing the release of key information, they can keep sellers, buyers, and competitors in the dark about their true intentions.

Tactics of Information Asymmetry in High-Stakes Negotiation

Controlling information is one of the most effective strategies in negotiation. The best dealmakers understand that the more the other party knows, the more leverage they have. By limiting access to key facts, disguising true intentions, and strategically revealing information at the right time, they shape negotiations in their favor before the other side even realizes what's happening.

Below are three case studies of how elite business leaders used information asymmetry to acquire assets at a fraction of their potential cost.

Stephen Ross:
Acquiring Hudson Yards Without Driving Up Prices

Stephen Ross, the billionaire real estate developer and founder of Related Companies, pulled off one of the most masterful land acquisition strategies in modern history when assembling the parcels for Hudson Yards in New York City. If landowners had realized they were selling to a developer planning a $25 billion mega-project, prices would have skyrocketed. Instead, Ross and his team used shell companies, intermediaries, and careful negotiation tactics to keep sellers in the dark.

How He Controlled Information:

- **Used Anonymous Buyers** – Instead of buying land directly through Related Companies, Ross used multiple LLCs and third-party buyers to acquire parcels over time. This prevented speculation and price inflation.

- **Downplayed Development Plans** – Whenever landowners inquired about future development, Ross's team would suggest small-scale projects instead of revealing the full vision. Sellers assumed they were parting with property for mid-tier commercial use, not a world-class mixed-use development.

- **Stretched Acquisitions Over Time** – Rather than making all acquisitions at once, Ross slowly assembled parcels **over several years**, keeping transactions quiet to avoid attention.

- **Leveraged City & Transit Deals** – Before making his final land purchases, Ross secured government commitments for subway expansion and rezoning that would massively increase the land's value—but he ensured these moves weren't made public until he had locked in deals.

Outcome:

Ross acquired large portions of the Hudson Yards land at a steep discount compared to what sellers could have demanded had they known its true future value. Once the project was publicly unveiled, land prices surged, but by then, Ross already controlled the critical pieces—turning a multi-billion dollar profit before the first skyscraper even broke ground.

Mark Zuckerberg:
Acquiring Instagram Without Overpaying

When Facebook acquired Instagram for $1 billion in 2012, most people believed Zuckerberg had simply identified a promising startup and made an aggressive offer. In reality, he used strategic misinformation and limited disclosure to keep

Instagram's founders from realizing how deeply Facebook planned to integrate—and ultimately dominate—the photo-sharing platform.

How He Controlled Information:

- **Kept Instagram's Leadership in the Dark** – Zuckerberg never revealed Facebook's internal data on how much Instagram was threatening its dominance in mobile photo-sharing. The company had already conducted internal studies showing Instagram could become a massive competitor, but this was never disclosed to Instagram's founders.

- **Acted Like an Ally, Not a Buyer** – Before making the offer, Zuckerberg framed his conversations with Instagram CEO Kevin Systrom as mentorship and industry advice, rather than an impending acquisition negotiation. This created a false sense of security.

- **Prevented a Bidding War** – Facebook approached Instagram before they could raise another round of venture capital, ensuring that competing investors like Google and Twitter didn't have a chance to drive up the price.

- **Promised Independence—Then Changed Course** – Zuckerberg assured Instagram's founders that the platform would operate separately under Facebook, which encouraged them to accept a lower offer. After the deal closed, Instagram was gradually absorbed into Facebook's ecosystem, reducing the original founders' control and financial upside.

Outcome:

Despite initial criticism that Facebook had overpaid, Instagram went on to become one of the most profitable acquisitions in tech history, generating billions in advertising revenue and cementing Facebook's dominance in social media. Had Instagram's founders known how much leverage they actually had, they could have negotiated a far higher valuation or structured a deal that allowed them to maintain more control

Deliberate Misinformation

Using Misinformation as a Negotiation Weapon

Misinformation is a strategic tool used by powerful dealmakers to shape the actions of competitors, sellers, and investors. Unlike simply hiding information, this tactic involves deliberately feeding misleading or incomplete facts to create a reaction that benefits the negotiator. The goal is to influence decisions in a way that makes the other party act out of fear, urgency, or miscalculation, giving the negotiator greater control over the deal.

Many of the world's top billionaires, investment firms, and corporate executives have mastered the art of planting selective or distorted information to manipulate markets, lower acquisition costs, or increase the value of their own assets before selling. Below are three major ways misinformation is used to gain a financial edge.

Rupert Murdoch: Use of Fake Acquisition Rumors to Boost Stock Prices

Rupert Murdoch, the billionaire media mogul behind News Corp and Fox, is notorious for manipulating financial markets through strategic misinformation. One of his most effective tactics has been leaking false or exaggerated acquisition rumors to drive up stock prices before selling shares or using them as collateral for new deals.

How He Used Misinformation to Profit

- **Murdoch Planted Buyout Rumors to Increase Stock Value**

  ▷ Before making key sales of his own media holdings, Murdoch ensured that reports of potential acquisitions would hit the financial press.

▷ These leaks created speculation that his companies were in high demand, attracting more investors and driving up stock prices.

▷ Once the share price had inflated due to the false narrative, he sold at a peak valuation before reality caught up.

- **Used Media Influence to Shape the Narrative**

  ▷ Unlike most corporate executives, Murdoch had an added advantage: he controlled the newspapers, TV stations, and online platforms that could spread his own misinformation.

  ▷ His network of journalists, analysts, and media executives ensured that even baseless rumors were reported as credible news.

  ▷ By the time the truth was revealed, Murdoch had already executed his financial moves.

- **Created Artificial Bidding Wars**

  ▷ In some cases, Murdoch would leak that multiple companies were competing to acquire one of his media assets, forcing real buyers to increase their offers.

  ▷ This tactic made companies overpay for assets that were never as competitive as they believed.

  ▷ The resulting deal ensured Murdoch extracted maximum value before market forces corrected the price.

Outcome

- Murdoch used misinformation to inflate the stock prices of his own companies, allowing him to sell at high valuations before prices stabilized.

- Competitors were frequently tricked into overbidding for media assets, believing they were competing in a heated market when they were actually playing into his strategy.

- Investors who reacted to Murdoch's leaked rumors without verifying facts often ended up buying shares at inflated prices, only to lose money when the hype faded.

Real Estate Developers
Spreading False Zoning Change Stories

In real estate, misinformation can be used to drive urgency, panic, or inflated pricing, often benefiting developers who are trying to buy land at lower prices or sell property at a premium. One of the most common tactics involves spreading false stories about impending zoning changes that force sellers or buyers into making rushed decisions.

How Developers Use Misinformation to Their Advantage

- **Creating Fear of Zoning Restrictions to Force Quick Sales**

  ▷ Developers looking to acquire land at low prices often spread rumors that zoning changes are about to restrict building rights.

  ▷ This misinformation scares property owners into selling quickly before the "restrictions" supposedly take effect.

  ▷ The developer then buys the land at a discount, knowing the zoning changes were never real or would not impact their plans.

- **Leaking False Stories of Rezoning to Drive Up Prices**

  ▷ On the flip side, when developers want to sell land or buildings, they sometimes leak information that zoning changes will increase property values.

  ▷ This tactic creates urgency among buyers who believe they are getting in before the market jumps in price.

▷ After selling at a premium, the developer exits the deal before buyers realize the zoning changes will not materialize.

- **Playing Local Politics to Spread Misinformation**

  ▷ Developers often plant stories in local newspapers or community meetings about upcoming regulations or incentives that favor their deals.

  ▷ By the time real information is released, developers have already secured their purchases or offloaded assets at premium prices.

Real-World Example:
Eduardo Costantini – The Billionaire Developer Who Mastered Market Perception

Eduardo Costantini, the Argentine billionaire behind Nordelta, built his real estate empire by strategically influencing market perceptions. His approach demonstrates how developers use misinformation to acquire land at lower prices, sell at peak valuations, and manipulate local sentiment for maximum profitability.

How Eduardo Costantini and Nordelta Fit the Model

- **Creating Fear of Zoning Restrictions to Force Quick Sales**

  ▷ In the late 1990s, Costantini needed to acquire large tracts of land from small farmers and landowners for his Nordelta project. Many were hesitant to sell.

  ▷ Rumors circulated that new environmental restrictions could soon limit large-scale development in the area. These restrictions were said to include wetlands protections and higher rural land taxes.

▷ Fearing their land might soon become undevelopable or heavily taxed, landowners sold quickly, often at steep discounts. Costantini's firm, Consultatio, secured thousands of acres at below-market rates.

- **Leaking False Stories of Rezoning to Drive Up Prices**

▷ As Nordelta took shape, speculation about the area's growth potential increased.

▷ Developers and insiders began hinting at future government-backed infrastructure projects, including new highways, expanded commuter rail, and tax incentives for businesses.

▷ These projects were discussed but were often exaggerated in scale or timeline.

▷ Believing the area was on the verge of a major real estate boom, buyers rushed in, paying inflated prices for Nordelta properties. Costantini's firm sold off parcels at peak valuations before many of these promised improvements materialized.

- **Playing Local Politics to Spread Misinformation**

▷ Costantini leveraged strong political connections to ensure favorable policies for Nordelta while competitors faced delays.

▷ His team strategically leaked information about potential new development restrictions elsewhere, driving buyer interest toward Nordelta.

▷ When political opposition to luxury gated communities grew, Costantini publicly supported initiatives like schools and mixed-use spaces. These gestures came only after Nordelta was fully developed and its property values had risen significantly.

Outcome

- Landowners sold their property at discounted prices due to fear of restrictive zoning changes.

- Developers sold properties at a premium by fueling speculation about future rezoning benefits that never materialized.

- Buyers, thinking they were ahead of the market, overpaid for properties, while Costantini and his firm exited at peak value.

Costantini's Nordelta strategy is a clear example of how developers can control market perception, use misinformation to create urgency, and leverage political influence to outmaneuver competitors. In high-stakes real estate, controlling information is just as valuable as controlling land

Investment Banks
Manipulating Valuation Figures to Mislead Competitors

During corporate buyouts and mergers, investment banks play a major role in shaping market sentiment through financial projections and valuation estimates. Sometimes, they intentionally spread misleading valuation figures to influence investor decisions, discourage rival buyers, or create temporary stock volatility.

How Investment Banks Use Misinformation in Mergers and Acquisitions

- **Overstating Valuations to Discourage Rival Buyers**

    ▷ When a major corporation is being sold, investment banks representing the seller often exaggerate revenue forecasts and growth projections.

    ▷ This misinformation makes the company appear more expensive than it really is, discouraging competitors from bidding.

▷ By the time accurate numbers emerge, the favored buyer has already locked in a deal.

- **Undervaluing Target Companies to Lower Buyout Prices**

  ▷ On the opposite end, investment banks working for buyers may leak negative financial reports about a target company to lower its stock price before making an acquisition offer.

  ▷ This tactic creates doubt among investors and weakens the target company's negotiating position.

  ▷ Once the deal is secured at a lower price, the buyer reveals better-than-expected financials, sending stock prices soaring.

- **Manipulating Earnings Estimates Before Deals Are Finalized**

  ▷ Before a merger, investment banks sometimes adjust earnings estimates up or down to control investor sentiment.

  ▷ If they want to push a deal forward, they inflate expectations to generate hype around the acquisition.

  ▷ If they want to kill a deal or lower the price, they quietly downgrade financial outlooks, scaring shareholders into accepting worse terms.

Outcome

- Competitors are misled into thinking a company is too expensive to pursue, allowing the preferred buyer to acquire it uncontested.

- Target companies lose bargaining power because their stock price has been artificially depressed before negotiations.

- Investors make decisions based on false valuation estimates, leading to financial losses when real numbers are revealed

Hiding True Intentions

Disguising Intentions in Negotiations – How the Best Dealmakers Keep Opponents in the Dark

One of the most powerful tactics in negotiation is never revealing your true intentions until it is too late for the other side to react effectively. The best dealmakers don't announce their plans in advance; instead, they use strategic misdirection, third-party intermediaries, and deliberate downplaying to keep opponents unaware of their ultimate goals.

By the time sellers, investors, or competitors realize what is happening, the deal is already structured in favor of the negotiator, leaving the other party with no leverage to fight back. This approach allows the most powerful business leaders to acquire assets at a discount, eliminate competition before it materializes, and control industries without opposition.

How Blackstone Uses Subsidiaries and Shell Companies to Conceal Takeovers

Blackstone, one of the world's largest private equity firms, has mastered the art of acquiring entire industries without sellers realizing who they are negotiating with. Instead of making direct bids under the Blackstone name, the firm uses subsidiaries, shell corporations, and third-party investors to quietly acquire pieces of a market before launching a full-scale takeover.

How Blackstone Controls Acquisitions Without Alerting Sellers

- **Using multiple entities to avoid detection**
  Blackstone rarely purchases all assets at once or under its own name. Instead, it creates multiple limited liability companies (LLCs) or acquires assets through independent investment groups. This prevents sellers from realizing that their competitors or peers are selling to the same entity.

- **Deliberately spreading out acquisitions over time**
  Instead of making one large, high-profile purchase, Blackstone acquires companies in small, unconnected transactions. This keeps sellers from recognizing a trend and raising their prices accordingly. By the time competitors or industry insiders notice a pattern, Blackstone already controls a dominant market position.

- **Launching the takeover only after securing critical assets**
  Once Blackstone has acquired a significant portion of an industry's key assets—whether it's real estate, technology firms, or healthcare providers—it announces its ownership publicly. At this point, competitors and sellers have no way to counter the move, as the market shift has already happened behind the scenes.

Example: Blackstone's Takeover of the Single-Family Rental Market

In the years following the 2008 financial crisis, Blackstone identified an opportunity in the housing market. Instead of openly buying thousands of homes under the Blackstone name, the firm:

- Created Invitation Homes, a subsidiary that appeared to be an independent property investment company.

- Used dozens of LLCs to purchase homes quietly, preventing sellers from realizing that institutional investors were entering the single-family rental market.

- Acquired tens of thousands of homes across the U.S. before the media or competitors recognized what was happening.

By the time the housing market stabilized and competitors tried to enter the space, Blackstone already controlled one of the largest rental home portfolios in the country.

Amazon's Strategy of
Downplaying Interest in Key Industries Before Dominating Them

Amazon has used a different but equally effective strategy to gain control over industries without alerting competitors or regulators. Instead of making aggressive acquisitions from the beginning, Amazon downplays its interest in certain sectors, publicly stating that it has no plans to expand into those markets. Then, once the industry is unprepared, Amazon moves in aggressively, acquiring key assets before anyone can react.

How Amazon Keeps Industries Unprepared for Its Expansions

- **Publicly denies interest in a market**
  Amazon has repeatedly stated that it has "no immediate plans" to enter various industries, lulling competitors into complacency. Many companies have mistakenly believed that Amazon would not become a direct competitor, only to be blindsided when the company moved in.

- **Builds silent infrastructure before making a major move**
  Before entering an industry, Amazon works behind the scenes to develop the infrastructure it needs to dominate. This includes acquiring warehouses, supply chains, and technology companies that seem unrelated to retail expansion.

- **Announces major acquisitions only after securing dominance**
  Once Amazon has enough infrastructure in place to rapidly scale, it announces its full commitment to an industry, leaving competitors with no time to develop a counter-strategy.

Example: Amazon's Expansion into Logistics and Shipping

For years, Amazon publicly claimed it had no interest in becoming a direct competitor to major shipping companies like UPS and FedEx. However, behind the scenes, it:

- Acquired small regional delivery companies and integrated them into its own logistics network.

- Quietly built a fleet of Amazon-branded delivery vans, allowing it to bypass UPS and FedEx for last-mile deliveries.

- Developed its own air cargo fleet, reducing reliance on external carriers.

By the time UPS and FedEx realized Amazon was serious about logistics, it was too late—Amazon had already built a shipping empire that could operate independently, forcing legacy shipping companies to scramble to adjust.

Michael Dell's Secret
Buyout Strategy to Take Dell Technologies Private

Michael Dell executed one of the most carefully planned corporate buyouts in history when he took Dell Technologies private in 2013. Instead of openly stating his plans, Dell intentionally misled investors about the company's future while secretly structuring a deal that would allow him to take full control at a discounted price.

How Michael Dell Hid His True Intentions Until It Was Too Late

- **Downplayed his buyout interest while quietly securing financing**
  Dell initially denied any plans to take the company private, keeping investors unaware of his long-term strategy. Meanwhile, he worked behind the scenes to secure financing from

private equity firms and structure a deal before announcing anything publicly.

- **Allowed shareholders to believe they had nego-tiating power**
  To avoid investor backlash, Dell let shareholders believe they were influencing the terms of the buyout. However, by the time they realized the full structure of the deal, it was already too late to mount an effective opposition.

- **Structured the deal to benefit himself personally**
  Dell negotiated preferential terms for himself, ensuring that even after the company went private, he retained maximum control while minimizing personal financial risk.

Outcome of the Dell Buyout

- Investors underestimated Dell's long-term strategy and agreed to a deal that benefited him far more than them.

- By the time shareholders recognized how undervalued the company was, Dell had already locked in the buyout at a favorable price.

- He later relisted Dell Technologies at a significantly higher valuation, proving that the original buyout was structured entirely to benefit him.

Key Takeaways

- **Never reveal your true intentions too early**

  ▷ If the other side knows your endgame, they will adjust their negotiation strategy to maximize their position.

  ▷ Keeping your real goals hidden allows you to control the timing, pricing, and structure of the deal.

- **Use intermediaries and third parties to avoid detection**

▷ Whether through shell companies, separate business units, or independent investors, breaking up acquisitions into smaller transactions keeps competitors from realizing what's happening.

- **Disarm competitors by publicly denying interest in a market**

  ▷ Making it seem like you are not a serious player in an industry creates a false sense of security for competitors, giving you time to prepare for a major move.

- **Ensure all critical assets are secured before making a major announcement**

  ▷ By the time the market realizes what is happening, you should already have enough control to prevent effective resistance.

- **Control the exit strategy before others realize what's at stake**

  ▷ Whether it's relisting a company after taking it private or locking in key supply chains before competitors react, the best dealmakers **ensure that** they win before the other side even understands the full scope of the deal

Preemptive Market Manipulation

Manipulating the Market Before Entering a Deal – Controlling Perception for Maximum Advantage

One of the most powerful strategies in high-stakes negotiations is shaping the market before making a move. By manipulating public perception, market sentiment, and competitor expectations, top negotiators ensure they enter a deal with maximum leverage. This tactic is used by billionaire investors, private equity firms, and corporate leaders to create conditions that force the other side into a weaker position before they even realize a negotiation is taking place.

Rather than reacting to market forces, elite dealmakers manufacture market conditions that benefit them. This includes controlling financial narratives, strategically timing announcements, influencing investor confidence, and even artificially depressing the value of an acquisition target to lower its purchase price. The key is ensuring that by the time the real transaction is happening, the outcome is already weighted in their favor.

Ken Griffin at Citadel –
Gathering Market Intelligence Before Major Investments

Ken Griffin, the billionaire founder of Citadel, has built one of the most powerful hedge funds in the world by ensuring that he always has more information than the competition before making investment decisions. His strategy revolves around gathering intelligence on market sentiment, institutional activity, and financial data before making a move, giving him a significant edge.

How Ken Griffin Uses Market Intelligence to Stay Ahead

- **Monitoring Market Sentiment Before Large Investments**
  Citadel employs advanced data analytics and artificial intelligence to track investor sentiment in real-time. Griffin does not wait for public market reports—his firm is often ahead of the news cycle, using internal modeling to predict trends before they are widely known.

- **Using High-Frequency Trading to Spot Market Movements**
  Citadel's high-frequency trading systems allow the firm to detect shifts in buying and selling pressure milliseconds before the broader market reacts. This enables Griffin to place trades at the most favorable moment, locking in gains before prices adjust.

- **Influencing Market Perception Before Taking Large Positions**
  Before making a major investment, Citadel sometimes places smaller trades or engages in market commentary to subtly influence investor sentiment. If Griffin wants to acquire a stock at a lower price, he may quietly short-sell shares or strategically leak skepticism about a company's future.

- **Forcing Competitors Into Unfavorable Positions**
  By creating a temporary wave of pessimism or enthusiasm around a stock, Citadel can force other hedge funds to over-react and take positions that ultimately benefit Griffin's long-term strategy. This ensures that Citadel's real move is always made after shaping the conditions to be most favorable.

Outcome of Griffin's Market Manipulation Strategy

- Citadel consistently enters and exits markets at the most profitable moments, ensuring superior returns.

- By gathering better intelligence than competitors, Griffin avoids riskier investments and makes moves before the broader market catches on.

- Other investors often fall into market traps created by Citadel, reacting to shifts that were strategically manufactured.

Private Equity Firms
Depressing Stock Prices Before a Buyout

Private equity firms are known for their aggressive and strategic tactics when acquiring companies at the lowest possible price. One of the most effective ways they achieve this is by artificially driving down the value of a target company before making a buyout offer. This allows them to acquire assets at a discount while ensuring minimal competition.

How Private Equity Firms Drive Down Target Company Stock Prices

- **Short-Selling Before Announcing Buyout Intentions**
  Many private equity firms place short positions on the stock of a company they intend to acquire. This creates downward pressure on the share price, making it appear that investors are losing confidence in the company's future.

- **Leaking Negative Market Sentiment**
  By subtly spreading concerns about a company's financial health or industry outlook, private equity firms can create a temporary panic. News stories or analyst reports discussing potential risks often trigger institutional investors to sell off shares, further depressing the stock price.

- **Waiting for the Right Moment to Make an Offer**
  Once the stock has dropped to an artificially low level, the private equity firm steps in as a "rescuer" and offers to buy the company at what appears to be a fair price. In reality, they are purchasing at a significant discount compared to its real potential value.

- **Using Legal and Financial Maneuvers to Weaken the Target Company's Position**
  In some cases, private equity firms will engage in strategic litigation, regulatory challenges, or corporate governance disputes to create uncertainty around a company's stock, driving prices lower before making an offer..

Outcome of This Strategy

- Target companies sell at artificially low prices, benefiting only the acquiring private equity firm.

- Public shareholders lose out, believing a company is failing when it is actually being manipulated.

- Competitors often misjudge a firm's valuation and fail to place competing bids.

Bill Gates' Early Microsoft Deals –
Creating the Illusion of Market Dominance

Bill Gates built Microsoft into a tech empire by using strategic partnerships, licensing agreements, and public perception tactics to make the company appear indispensable to customers, suppliers, and investors before negotiations even started. His ability to shape the industry narrative before making a deal ensured that Microsoft was always in a position of power.

How Bill Gates Manipulated Market Perception to Strengthen Microsoft's Position

- **Pre-Announcing Deals That Weren't Finalized**
  Microsoft frequently announced partnerships, software integrations, and licensing deals before they were actually secured. This created the perception that Microsoft was the dominant force in computing, making suppliers and partners feel they had no choice but to work with the company.

- **Locking in Industry Standards Before Competitors Could Respond**
  Gates pushed Microsoft's software into businesses and government agencies before competitors could establish their own platforms. Once Microsoft became the standard, it was nearly impossible for rivals to displace them.

- **Using Exclusive Licensing to Block Competition**
  Microsoft signed deals with PC manufacturers requiring them to bundle Windows with their products, ensuring that competitors had no distribution channels left.

- **Convincing Investors That Microsoft Was an Inevitable Winner**

By constantly feeding media stories about Microsoft's dominance, Gates ensured that investors saw the company as the future of computing. This created a self-fulfilling prophecy where capital and talent flowed to Microsoft while starving competitors.

Outcome of Gates' Strategy

- Microsoft secured massive licensing deals before competitors could even react, locking them out of key markets.

- Investors poured money into Microsoft, believing in its inevitable success, which further strengthened its negotiating power.

- Rival tech companies were often forced to follow Microsoft's lead rather than challenge it directly.

Key Takeaways

- **The best deals are won before negotiations even start**

  ▷ By manipulating market perception, top dealmakers ensure they enter negotiations from a position of strength.

- **Shaping public and investor sentiment creates leverage**

  ▷ Whether by short-selling, planting strategic news stories, or pre-announcing partnerships, controlling the narrative forces others to react to you rather than the other way around.

- **Competitors and sellers make mistakes when they act on manipulated information**

  ▷ Many investors, sellers, and industry leaders **fall into traps created by misinformation**, leading them to sell too low or miss opportunities entirely.

- **The ability to move before others recognize your true strategy is a key advantage**

  ▷ The longer you can keep your real intentions hidden, the more control you have over how the market responds to your moves

Case Study:
How Larry Ellison Bought a $500M Company for Pennies

Larry Ellison, the billionaire founder of Oracle, executed one of the most brutal takeovers in tech history when he acquired PeopleSoft. His strategy revolved entirely around controlling the flow of information and manipulating shareholder perception.

- **Step 1: Lowering the Target's Value**

  ▷ Before making an official offer, Ellison launched a public disinformation campaign questioning the long-term viability of PeopleSoft.

  ▷ He suggested that Oracle was considering exiting the market segment PeopleSoft operated in, discouraging other potential buyers.

  ▷ Oracle's legal team filed vague antitrust concerns with regulatory bodies, creating uncertainty about PeopleSoft's ability to survive.

- **Step 2: Strategic Offer Timing**

  ▷ Once PeopleSoft's stock plummeted due to uncertainty, Ellison moved in with an underpriced offer.

  ▷ The initial bid was so low that it seemed like a joke, but it set the negotiating anchor, forcing PeopleSoft's board to negotiate from a weakened position.

- **Step 3: Divide and Conquer**

  ▷ Ellison turned PeopleSoft's shareholders against their own board, leaking information that suggested rejecting Oracle's offer would cause a further drop in stock price.

  ▷ He targeted key investors directly, convincing them that PeopleSoft's leadership was incapable of negotiating in their best interest.

- **Step 4: The Final Squeeze**

  ▷ As PeopleSoft's stock price remained volatile, Ellison continued spreading misinformation about whether Oracle was still interested in the deal, keeping investors anxious.

  ▷ He then reduced his offer slightly, claiming that the company's performance had deteriorated—forcing the board into a desperate acceptance.

In the end, Oracle bought PeopleSoft for far less than its peak value, and Ellison walked away owning a major competitor for pennies on the dollar.

Key Takeaways for Negotiators

- **The first move in a negotiation should always involve controlling information.** If the other side knows everything you do, you've already lost leverage.

- **Never reveal your true intentions** until the deal is locked in. Let the other party think they're winning while you shape the outcome behind the scenes.

- **Use misinformation and market manipulation carefully.** A well-placed rumor or misleading leak can shift millions—or billions—in your favor.

- **Target shareholders, stakeholders, and outside influencers.** Sometimes, the best way to control a negotiation is by swaying those **around** the decision-makers.

- **Set the price anchor early, even if it's extreme.** The first number in a negotiation often dictates how the rest of the deal unfolds.

Final Thought

Information is the most valuable currency in any negotiation. **Those who control it dictate the terms.** While others waste time arguing over price, elite dealmakers manipulate data, perception, and timing to **win the deal before it even starts.**

CHAPTER 5:

The Art of the Psychological Squeeze –
Making the Other Side Feel Trapped

Negotiation is not just about financial terms, contracts, or legal agreements—it is about psychological dominance. The best dealmakers understand that emotions often dictate decisions more than logic. When an opponent feels trapped, overwhelmed, or pressured, they make mistakes and concede more than they otherwise would.

The psychological squeeze is the art of applying pressure so effectively that the other party sees no viable alternative but to accept your terms. This is achieved through a combination of subtle mental manipulation, strategic delays, emotional exhaustion, and public pressure. The goal is to make the other party feel as though walking away is impossible and continuing to negotiate on your terms is the only logical escape.

Tactics for Psychological Domination

Mirroring and Manipulation – *Bill Gates'*
Strategy for Forcing Rivals Into No-Win Situations

One of the most effective ways to trap competitors into self-destructive behavior is to mirror their moves, forcing them into costly and unsustainable races. Bill Gates mastered this during

Microsoft's early years, frequently using this technique to bleed competitors dry before securing dominant market positions.

- **Adopting competitor strategies to force wasteful spending**
  Gates often mimicked the strategies of rival companies just enough to force them to pour money into unprofitable ventures. By copying their product launches, pricing models, and marketing tactics, Microsoft made competitors believe they needed to double down on costly initiatives to maintain their market position. Many of these companies were financially weaker than Microsoft, meaning Gates could afford to play the long game while they burned through capital.

- **Creating the illusion of an unwinnable battle**
  Microsoft would signal aggressive expansion into new markets, forcing competitors to divert funds away from core operations to fight a war they were not prepared for. The mere threat of Microsoft entering a market often caused competitors to panic and overspend, even if Microsoft had no real intention of committing fully.

- **Outcome of this strategy**
  Gates used this strategy to drive Netscape, WordPerfect, and other software competitors into submission, leading Microsoft to dominate operating systems, office software, and internet browsers. Microsoft was often able to outlast competitors not because of superior products, but because it controlled the financial war of attrition.

Anchoring Expectations –
Elon Musk's High-Stakes Negotiation Bluffing

Anchoring is a psychological strategy where a negotiator sets an extreme starting position in order to make subsequent compromises seem reasonable. Elon Musk has mastered this in business deals, salary negotiations, and corporate takeovers.

- **Setting outrageous initial demands**
  Musk frequently sets unrealistic opening demands in negotiations, making any later compromise feel like a victory for
  the other side—even when he still gets what he truly wanted.
  When negotiating funding or production terms for Tesla and
  SpaceX, Musk has been known to ask for terms that seem
  so extreme that even a significant reduction still leaves him
  with a highly favorable deal.

- **Creating a false sense of compromise**
  Investors, regulators, and suppliers often feel like they "win"
  negotiations because Musk eventually lowers his demands—
  without realizing they are still giving him a major advantage.
  When Tesla negotiated subsidies and tax incentives, Musk
  asked for massive breaks, allowing him to "settle" for lower,
  yet still massive, incentives.

- **Outcome of this strategy**
  Musk secured billions in tax breaks and government subsidies
  by initially demanding numbers so high that even a reduced
  figure was a massive win for him. This tactic also played out
  in his Twitter acquisition, where he initially made aggressive
  demands before "compromising," only to still close the deal
  at a highly beneficial valuation.

Public Embarrassment –
How Jerry Jones Forces Sports Networks into Higher Deals

Public image is one of the most underestimated weapons in
negotiation. Jerry Jones, the billionaire owner of the Dallas Cowboys, is notorious for using public perception and media pressure
to force opponents into submission.

- **Leaking partial deal details to the press**
  Jones has strategically leaked partial details of negotiation
  discussions with sports networks to stir public outrage and
  force networks into unfavorable deals. When negotiating TV

rights for the NFL and Dallas Cowboys games, Jones ensured that networks felt fan and advertiser pressure before the deals were finalized.

- **Using fan outrage to strengthen his position**
  If negotiations were not going in his favor, Jones would publicly suggest that networks were being unreasonable, making it appear as though fans might lose access to Cowboys games. This forced networks to concede higher payouts because they feared fan backlash, lost advertising revenue, and a tarnished brand image.

- **Outcome of this strategy**
  Jones negotiated some of the most lucrative sports media deals in history, ensuring that the Cowboys receive premium exposure and revenue. Networks often end up paying more than they originally intended just to avoid bad public relations and disputes.

Forced Fatigue –
Mark Cuban's Strategy of Draining the Opposition

Mark Cuban, the billionaire investor and owner of the Dallas Mavericks, understands that negotiating while exhausted leads to poor decisions. One of his most effective tactics is deliberately stretching negotiations late into the night, knowing that fatigue weakens the other party's ability to think clearly.

- **Extending negotiation hours until the opposition makes mistakes**
  Cuban drags out meetings for hours beyond what is necessary, forcing the other side to negotiate when they are physically and mentally drained. Most people want to end a negotiation just to get some rest, which leads to hurried decision-making and unnecessary concessions.

- **Keeping his own team energized while the other side weakens**
  Cuban ensures his team is prepared for long sessions, while the opposition often does not plan for extended hours. This leads to situations where the other party's negotiators agree to terms they might not have under normal circumstances.

- **Outcome of this strategy**
  Cuban has secured better ownership deals, sponsorship agreements, and TV rights by exhausting the opposition into submission. Business rivals often give in just to conclude the meeting, without realizing how much they have given away.

Case Study:
How Dan Gilbert Secured a Billion-Dollar Tax Break Through Bureaucratic Exhaustion

Dan Gilbert, the billionaire owner of Quicken Loans and the Cleveland Cavaliers, demonstrated one of the most effective negotiation strategies when seeking a massive tax break for his downtown Detroit projects. Instead of negotiating the financial terms head-on, he weaponized bureaucracy by overwhelming city officials with excessive paperwork, meetings, and legal complexity. This strategy, known as bureaucratic exhaustion, is designed to make the process so tedious and time-consuming that the opposing side eventually gives in just to move forward.

Rather than pressuring city officials directly, Gilbert's team created a never-ending maze of reports, legal filings, and bureaucratic delays, forcing officials to engage in an exhausting, drawn-out process. As time dragged on, businesses and residents became increasingly frustrated with the delays, putting additional pressure on the city to resolve the matter. Eventually, Gilbert's relentless strategy wore officials down, and they granted him a massive tax incentive package simply to move past the negotiations.

Flooding City Off ith Paperwork and Meetings

One of the core elements of Gilbert's strategy was to bury city officials in administrative complexity. His team understood that city governments operate under strict timelines, finite resources, and bureaucratic constraints. By exploiting these weaknesses, Gilbert shifted the balance of power in his favor.

- His legal and financial teams submitted an overwhelming volume of reports, applications, and financial projections, making it nearly impossible for city officials to quickly review or process them.

- Whenever the city requested additional details or clarifications, Gilbert's team provided even more extensive and highly technical reports, further slowing the process.

- Officials who may have originally been inclined to negotiate on equal footing found themselves trapped in an endless cycle of reviewing, analyzing, and requesting more documents, pushing negotiations further into gridlock.

- The sheer volume of materials meant that every new discussion required extensive backtracking, delaying the process even further and exhausting city officials.

By leveraging bureaucratic red tape, Gilbert controlled the pace of negotiations and ensured that city officials spent more time buried in paperwork than actually negotiating the financial terms of the deal.

Dragging the Process Out Until the City Had No Other Option

Once negotiations were thoroughly bogged down, Gilbert's team used time itself as a weapon. While bureaucrats were forced to navigate his mountains of paperwork, external factors began adding pressure on city officials to make a decision.

- As the process stalled for months, public frustration grew among local businesses, investors, and residents, who were eager to see economic revitalization in downtown Detroit.

- City officials, facing pressure from business owners and community leaders, became increasingly desperate to finalize the deal, fearing backlash for holding up development.

- By creating artificial urgency through delays that were entirely within his team's control, Gilbert ensured that when the city finally wanted to move forward, it was on his terms.

- City officials, now overwhelmed and eager to avoid further delays, were left with two choices: continue down the never-ending bureaucratic path or approve Gilbert's tax incentives and move forward.

The longer Gilbert dragged out the process, the more city officials felt they were being seen as obstructionists rather than negotiators. Eventually, the frustration of local businesses and the desire to showcase Detroit's redevelopment efforts outweighed the city's willingness to push back on Gilbert's tax incentive requests.

Outcome of This Strategy

- Gilbert successfully secured a billion-dollar tax incentive package without making major financial concessions.

- City officials, worn down by the process, granted him the deal simply to put an end to the bureaucratic nightmare.

- The city lost out on the ability to negotiate a more favorable tax structure, potentially costing millions in lost revenue over time.

- The precedent set by Gilbert's strategy made it easier for other developers to demand similar incentives, as the city had established a pattern of conceding under pressure.

Why This Strategy Works

Gilbert's approach highlights a fundamental principle in negotiation—exhaustion is just as effective as financial leverage. By making the negotiation process unbearable, he ensured that city officials prioritized getting the deal done over getting the best deal possible.

This tactic works particularly well against bureaucratic institutions, government entities, and large organizations that operate under strict timelines and public scrutiny. Many officials and executives would rather close a deal with suboptimal terms than face prolonged uncertainty, scrutiny, and public criticism for inaction.

Final Thought

Dan Gilbert's strategy was not about outbidding competitors or presenting the most compelling financial argument—it was about winning through sheer persistence and calculated bureaucracy. By using paperwork as a weapon and creating frustration among city officials, he made it easier for them to grant his demands than to continue fighting. His ability to manipulate the negotiation process itself ultimately allowed him to secure a billion-dollar tax incentive package with minimal resistanceTop of FormBottom of Form

Key Takeaways

- Controlling the speed of a negotiation is just as powerful as controlling the terms. Deliberate delays can create pressure on the other party to concede.

- Exploiting bureaucratic inefficiencies can wear down decision-makers, making them more likely to agree just to move forward. Most institutions are not equipped to handle prolonged and highly complex negotiations.

- Artificial urgency, when combined with public and internal pressure, forces the other side to prioritize completion over negotiating the best terms. By stretching out the process, Gilbert ensured that the city's focus shifted from the deal itself to just getting it done.

- Governments and large organizations are particularly vulnerable to bureaucratic exhaustion tactics. The larger the institution, the more paperwork, legal reviews, and delays they face—making them easier to overwhelm.

CHAPTER 6:

Weaponizing Relationships –
How Billionaires Use
Allies as Leverage

The most powerful negotiators do not act alone. They create alliances, cultivate insiders, and use strategic relationships to gain leverage before a deal even begins. While average negotiators rely on financial incentives or contractual terms, billionaires and industry leaders use people as their most valuable asset.

By pre-conditioning decision-makers, stacking the board with allies, and orchestrating external pressure, elite dealmakers ensure they have overwhelming influence before a formal offer is even on the table. The goal is simple: when negotiations start, the outcome has already been quietly decided in their favor.

Tactics for Leveraging Relationships

Third-Party Endorsements –
How Ian Schrager Uses Influence to Secure Funding

Ian Schrager, the legendary hotel developer and co-founder of Studio 54, has perfected the art of using high-profile relationships to make his deals almost impossible to reject. Unlike traditional developers who rely on financial projections and feasibility studies to convince lenders and investors, Schrager employs a more strategic approach—he builds an aura of exclusivity and cultural significance around his projects before they even break ground. By securing endorsements from celebrities, cultural icons, and industry tastemakers, he ensures that his developments are seen as much more than real estate deals—they become lifestyle movements.

This approach creates a sense of urgency among lenders, investors, and city officials, who fear missing out on the opportunity to be associated with Schrager's projects. The weight of high-profile endorsements shifts the conversation from whether his developments should be approved to how quickly they can be moved forward.

How Ian Schrager Uses Third-Party Endorsements to Influence Decision-Makers

- When Schrager plans a new hotel, he strategically involves top designers, musicians, artists, and fashion icons in the early stages of the project. By doing this, he turns the development into a cultural event rather than just another hospitality deal. Lenders and investors are not just looking at numbers; they are evaluating a project that has already generated excitement and visibility.

- Celebrities and influencers associated with Schrager's developments often publicly support and promote the project, creating buzz before the deal is even finalized. This kind of organic promotion makes it difficult for financial institutions to ignore the project, as its success already seems inevitable.

- Investors and lenders who might hesitate on a conventional hotel deal fear losing out on the prestige and marketing exposure that comes with Schrager's brand. This sense of exclusivity and cultural importance makes them more inclined to approve funding, even if the project carries higher risks.

- By securing endorsements and branding partnerships before he walks into negotiations, Schrager pre-sells the vision of his development. Decision-makers are not just evaluating a proposal—they are being invited to join a project that already feels successful.

Why This Strategy Works

Schrager understands that people, particularly those in finance and real estate, want to be associated with something groundbreaking. A hotel project with ordinary financial backing and projections is just another investment opportunity, but a development tied to the world's top designers, musicians, and influencers carries a cultural cachet that money alone cannot buy.

By the time Schrager officially presents his project to banks or investors, they are no longer looking at it as just a real estate deal. They are looking at it as a once-in-a-lifetime opportunity to attach their name to something iconic. The financials still matter, but they become secondary to the project's perceived cultural impact.

How Lenders and Investors React to Schrager's Tactics

- Many lenders are risk-averse and may hesitate to finance traditional hotel developments due to market saturation or economic uncertainty. However, when a project carries the backing of influential designers and celebrities, it is no longer viewed as a conventional business decision but as a branding opportunity.

- Investors who want media attention and high-profile networking opportunities are drawn to Schrager's projects. Even if the financial return is not significantly higher than other hospitality investments, the social capital gained from being associated with a Schrager property often outweighs the monetary risk.

- City officials who control permits and zoning approvals are also influenced by these high-profile endorsements. Approving a new hotel development can be a bureaucratic process, but if the project is framed as a transformative cultural hub that attracts global attention, approvals happen much faster.

Real-World Examples:
Schrager's Strategy

Schrager has repeatedly used this playbook throughout his career. When he launched the Edition Hotels brand in collaboration with Marriott, he involved leading designers and cultural influencers to create a sense of exclusivity. Even though Marriott had extensive resources to fund the project, Schrager's ability to turn the brand into a global phenomenon before the first hotel even opened was what made the deal so powerful.

Similarly, when he developed the Public Hotel in New York, Schrager positioned it as not just a place to stay, but a cultural destination. By involving key tastemakers and celebrities in the brand's early messaging, he ensured that media attention and investor enthusiasm were already in place before the project was completed.

The Psychological Impact on Decision-Makers

Lenders, investors, and government officials all face pressure in their decision-making processes. When a high-profile project already has public backing and media buzz, saying no becomes significantly harder. Decision-makers do not want to be seen as the ones who rejected an opportunity that could shape the future of an industry or a city.

By carefully curating relationships and endorsements before negotiations begin, Schrager ensures that the people sitting across the table from him feel a psychological pressure to approve the deal, not based on financials alone, but because they want to be part of something extraordinary.

Key Takeaways

* Creating cultural significance around a project before negotiations begin makes decision-makers feel they are joining a movement, not just approving a deal.

- Involving celebrities, designers, and cultural influencers early in a project's lifecycle shifts the perception from a financial transaction to a branding opportunity.

- Lenders and investors often fear missing out on high-profile, culturally relevant projects and will approve deals to avoid being left behind.

- Pre-selling a project's success before entering the boardroom ensures that negotiations are about logistics and execution, not about convincing people the deal is worth doing.

- City officials who may otherwise be hesitant to approve a project feel compelled to support it when it carries public momentum and influential endorsements.

Final Thought

Ian Schrager does not just develop hotels—he creates cultural landmarks that people want to be associated with. His ability to shape the perception of a project before negotiations even start is what makes him one of the most effective dealmakers in the hospitality industry. The lesson for any negotiator is clear: if you can make your project feel like an exclusive opportunity, decision-makers will want to be part of it, often on your terms.

Pre-Negotiation Conditioning —
How BlackRock Seeds Influence Before Making Offers

BlackRock, the world's largest asset manager, does not simply walk into negotiations hoping for a favorable outcome. Instead, it plants the seeds of influence months in advance, shaping industry sentiment and decision-maker attitudes long before the first formal meeting.

- Before attempting a major acquisition, BlackRock executives hold informal meetings with key industry figures, board members, and financial analysts. These conversations are designed to frame BlackRock's involvement as inevitable and beneficial.

- Board members of target companies often receive indirect exposure to BlackRock's perspective long before any offer is made, softening resistance and creating internal advocates.

- By the time an official proposal is submitted, many decision-makers have already been psychologically conditioned to view the deal favorably, making negotiations significantly easier.

This subtle yet highly effective strategy ensures that opposition is reduced before the real negotiation begins.

Building Political Favor –
How Jorge Perez Uses Government Ties to Secure Approvals

Jorge Perez, the billionaire real estate developer behind The Related Group, has mastered the art of using political relationships to gain a competitive advantage in real estate development. Unlike many developers who fight regulatory battles after submitting proposals, Perez ensures that government officials and key decision-makers are already aligned with his projects before they even enter the approval process.

His strategy is based on long-term relationship building, political engagement, and strategic community involvement. By embedding himself into the political and social fabric of the cities where he develops, Perez ensures that his projects face minimal resistance, move through bureaucratic red tape faster, and receive favorable treatment.

How Jorge Perez Embeds Himself in the Political Landscape

Investing in Community Partnerships to Build Trust and Influence

Perez understands that real estate development is not just about securing land and financing—it is also about shaping public perception and gaining community support. To achieve this, he actively invests in local initiatives and organizations that align with the interests of government leaders.

- He donates generously to local charities, educational programs, and housing initiatives that city officials publicly support, positioning himself as a champion of the community rather than just another developer.

- By funding cultural and civic programs, he creates goodwill that makes government officials more inclined to work with him when his projects require approvals.

- He serves on advisory boards and committees, ensuring that he has direct access to key political figures long before he needs anything from them.

These actions do not just make him a well-known figure in political circles—they create an environment where rejecting one of his projects could be seen as going against community interests.

Pre-Negotiation Lobbying – How Perez Gains Support Before Submitting Proposals

Perez does not wait until a project is ready to be presented before engaging with city officials. Instead, he **works behind the scenes to build support months or even years in advance**. By the time his development proposals are submitted, key decision-makers already understand how the project aligns with their goals.

- He initiates informal conversations with city planners, mayors, and zoning officials, positioning his projects as solutions to urban growth, economic expansion, and housing shortages.

- He ensures that his projects reflect the policy priorities of local governments, such as affordable housing, mixed-use developments, or public space enhancements, making it easier for officials to justify their support.

- Before official discussions take place, Perez leverages his network of influential lobbyists, community leaders, and local business figures to promote the benefits of his developments.

By embedding himself in conversations early, Perez prevents opposition from forming. Government officials and planning boards feel personally invested in the project's success, making them less likely to scrutinize or reject it.

Securing Behind-the-Scenes Endorsements Before Public Hearings

When real estate projects require city council or planning board approvals, many developers prepare for a fight. Perez, on the other hand, ensures that by the time a public hearing takes place, he has already secured the necessary support behind closed doors.

- He works with key political figures and urban planners well in advance, shaping the narrative of his projects as positive contributions to the city.

- He mobilizes community groups, business leaders, and local influencers to publicly endorse his proposals, creating the perception that his developments are widely supported.

- He minimizes resistance by personally engaging with potential opponents, addressing their concerns, and often incorporating small concessions that make them feel heard while keeping the core project intact.

By the time a vote is needed, the outcome is already largely decided. City officials who might have initially been hesitant now feel pressured to approve the project, knowing that rejecting it would mean going against influential supporters and missing out on promised community benefits.

Why This Strategy Works So Effectively

Perez's approach to political relationship-building works because it **transforms real estate negotiations from transactional battles into strategic collaborations**. Instead of simply presenting a project and hoping for approval, he ensures that his developments are framed as beneficial public initiatives from the start. His method is particularly effective because:

- **Government officials are incentivized to support projects that align with their political agendas.** When Perez's developments reflect the city's goals—such as creating jobs, improving infrastructure, or increasing housing—officials feel compelled to approve them.

- **By positioning himself as a long-term partner rather than an opportunistic developer,** Perez avoids the typical pushback from city councils and planning boards. Many developers only engage with city officials when they need something, whereas Perez nurtures relationships continuously, ensuring that when he does need approvals, they are much easier to obtain.

- **Community support is already in place before opposition can build.** Opponents of large-scale developments often organize to block projects, but Perez's ability to secure endorsements ahead of time minimizes resistance.

Examples of Jorge Perez's Political Influence in Action

Perez has used these strategies to develop some of the most high-profile real estate projects in Miami and beyond.

- When The Related Group sought approvals for luxury high-rise projects in Miami, Perez had already built relationships with city officials and local business groups. His long-standing community involvement made it difficult for regulators to reject his proposals, even when they faced criticism.

- During negotiations for large mixed-use developments, he ensured that his projects included public benefits such as parks, affordable housing units, and infrastructure improvements, making it politically advantageous for officials to approve them.

- Perez has maintained strong ties with mayors, commissioners, and planning boards in major cities, allowing him to bypass many of the bureaucratic hurdles that slow down other developers.

The Risks and Challenges of This Approach

While political relationship-building is a powerful tool, it also comes with challenges and risks that require careful navigation.

- **Regulatory scrutiny can increase if relationships appear too close.** If developers seem to be receiving preferential treatment, investigative journalists and watchdog groups may question whether approvals are being granted fairly.

- **Political shifts can impact influence.** A new administration with different priorities may not be as supportive of a developer's projects, making it important to diversify relationships rather than rely on a single political figure.

- **Balancing public perception is key.** While securing government support is essential, projects must still be seen as beneficial to the broader community. If a development is perceived as serving only corporate interests, public opposition can override political backing.

Key Takeaways for Negotiators

- Political influence is just as important as financial strength in real estate and large-scale business negotiations. Developers who understand how to navigate government relationships gain a massive advantage.

- Engaging with government leaders long before a project is proposed ensures that decision-makers already view it favorably, reducing resistance when approvals are needed.

- Investing in community partnerships and local initiatives creates goodwill that makes city officials more likely to support a developer's projects.

Ensuring that projects align with the policy goals of local governments makes it politically beneficial for officials to approve them.

Securing behind-the-scenes endorsements before public hearings makes opposition much harder to organize and sustain.

Final Thought

Jorge Perez's success is not just about building real estate—it is about **building relationships**. By embedding himself in the political landscape, securing community trust, and pre-negotiating approvals behind the scenes, he ensures that his projects move forward with minimal resistance. His strategy highlights a fundamental truth in high-stakes negotiations: **the most successful deals are often won before they are even formally proposed**.

Orchestrating a Rival Bid –
How Michael Dell Created Artificial Competition to Force a Deal

One of the most ruthless negotiation tactics is creating the illusion of competition to pressure decision-makers into accepting your terms. When Michael Dell wanted to take Dell Technologies private, he convinced Silver Lake, a major private equity firm, to place a rival bid—not because he wanted competition, but because he wanted leverage.

- By introducing Silver Lake as a competing bidder, Dell forced the company's shareholders to act quickly, fearing they might miss out on the best deal.

- This also discouraged other investors from attempting to block Dell's offer, as they assumed competition would drive the price higher.

- Once shareholders were sufficiently pressured, Dell secured the deal on his own terms, having used the rival bid purely as a negotiation tool.

This tactic is particularly useful in high-stakes acquisitions, where creating urgency can tip the balance in favor of the prepared negotiator.

Case Study:
How Robert Kraft Built a Sports and Business Empire Without Owning Everything

Robert Kraft, the billionaire owner of the New England Patriots, is a master of using relationships, alliances, and strategic positioning to gain control over high-value assets—often without having to own them outright. While his name is synonymous with NFL dominance, his rise to power was not through conventional sports team ownership alone. Instead, Kraft leveraged relationships with corporate leaders, politicians, and media executives to position himself as one of the most influential figures in professional sports, real estate, and media deals.

Much like Rupert Murdoch controlled media empires without majority ownership, Kraft built a massive sports and entertainment empire by mastering strategic partnerships, political lobbying, and corporate influence. By securing the right allies, he not only took control of the Patriots but also turned Gillette Stadium into a multi-billion-dollar real estate hub and positioned himself as a key decision-maker in sports media and broadcasting rights.

How Robert Kraft Used Relationships and Leverage to Secure Control

- **Winning the Patriots Without Overpaying for the Franchise**

  ▷ Kraft initially had no direct path to owning the New England Patriots. Instead of trying to buy the team outright, he first purchased the stadium lease rights in 1988, knowing that any future owner would have to deal with him.

  ▷ By securing the stadium lease, Kraft created leverage over team ownership, positioning himself as a necessary partner in any future sale.

  ▷ When the Patriots' then-owner, James Orthwein, wanted to move the team to St. Louis, Kraft used his lease control to block the relocation unless he was paid to release the lease—an option Orthwein couldn't afford.

  ▷ Orthwein was left with no real choice but to sell the team to Kraft in 1994, allowing Kraft to secure ownership for $172 million—a record at the time, but far less than what the team could have been worth had it moved to a major media market.

By using legal positioning and financial leverage, Kraft **controlled the Patriots long before he officially owned them**, forcing the deal in his favor without needing to outbid other potential buyers.

- **Turning Gillette Stadium Into a Real Estate Powerhouse**

  ▷ After securing the Patriots, Kraft understood that the stadium itself was more valuable than just a sports venue—it was a gateway to a real estate empire.

  ▷ Rather than simply upgrading the old Foxboro Stadium, he privately financed Gillette Stadium with limited public funding, ensuring that he retained full control of the revenue streams, sponsorships, and land surrounding it.

▷ Kraft's control of the stadium allowed him to expand beyond football, attracting concerts, corporate events, and entertainment venues that made the property valuable year-round.

▷ He negotiated key tax incentives and infrastructure deals with local and state governments to make the project viable, leveraging his political relationships to gain approvals and subsidies.

Through these moves, Kraft didn't just build a stadium—he turned it into a billion-dollar real estate hub, controlling entertainment revenue without ever having to own every aspect of the businesses operating within it.

Influencing NFL Decision-Making
and Media Rights Without Owning the League

- As a franchise owner, Kraft understood that the real power in sports came from media rights and league decision-making, not just team ownership.

- He built strong relationships with NFL executives, major broadcast networks, and corporate sponsors, positioning himself as a key figure in NFL television negotiations and expansion discussions.

- When the NFL was considering new television deals, Kraft played a crucial role in securing the lucrative $18 billion TV contract with CBS in 1998, which reshaped the financial structure of the league.

- By strengthening relationships with commissioners and media executives, Kraft ensured that the Patriots—and his business interests—were always positioned favorably in major league-wide decisions.

Through these relationships, Kraft wielded influence far beyond his role as an owner, shaping NFL policy, business expansions, and media negotiations that benefitted his own investments.

Why This Strategy Works So Effectively

Kraft's approach demonstrates that control and influence matter more than ownership. Rather than simply buying into existing opportunities, he created his own leverage points, secured key relationships, and forced negotiations to tilt in his favor before deals were even formalized.

His success can be attributed to several key factors:

- **Owning the infrastructure around the asset, rather than just the asset itself.** His control of stadium real estate gave him a level of power beyond team ownership.

- **Using strategic partnerships to avoid unnecessary financial risks.** By working with local governments, corporate sponsors, and media partners, Kraft ensured that his projects were always supported by external funding sources.

- **Leveraging legal and contractual positioning to dictate negotiations.** He forced the Patriots' sale to him by controlling the lease, a move that gave him power over the team's fate before he ever put in a bid.

- **Building alliances with decision-makers before major deals happen.** His relationships with NFL executives and media leaders ensured that he was always ahead of league-wide negotiations.

Key Takeaways for Negotiators

- **Ownership is not always necessary**—if you control the assets or infrastructure surrounding a deal, you can shape its outcome in your favor.

- **Pre-positioning yourself before negotiations** begin ensures that the other party has limited options, making them more likely to agree to your terms.

- **Political and corporate relationships are just as valuable as financial capital**, as they allow for approvals, funding, and strategic partnerships that competitors may lack.

- Controlling media relationships and sponsorship deals ensures that you have more influence over decision-making than simply being an asset owner.

- The best negotiators force their counterparts into a position where agreeing to the deal is the easiest or only viable option, as Kraft did when blocking the Patriots' relocation.

Final Thought

Robert Kraft's success is not just about owning a football team—it is about owning influence. By controlling key real estate, securing strong political and business relationships, and positioning himself at the center of NFL financial negotiations, Kraft built a billion-dollar empire without needing to own every asset outright. His approach proves that the most successful dealmakers do not just buy into opportunities—they create the conditions that make their dominance inevitable.

CHAPTER 7:

The Illusion of Concessions –
Making the Other Side Think They Won

The best negotiators do not just win a deal—they make the other side believe they won. This psychological trick reduces resistance, prevents future disputes, and allows negotiations to close with minimal friction. If a counterpart feels like they fought hard and walked away victorious, they are far less likely to question the outcome later.

Billionaires and elite dealmakers know that the perception of a good deal is often more important than the reality of one. By structuring negotiations to provide the illusion of significant concessions while still keeping control, they ensure that their long-term advantage remains intact. These tactics allow them to walk away with the most valuable parts of a deal while their opponents celebrate hollow victories.

Tactics for Giving False Concessions

Reversible Giveaways –
How Mark Zuckerberg Neutralizes Competition

Mark Zuckerberg is a master of giving up short-term advantages that he can take back later. Instead of outright denying competitors or partners the things they want, he grants them access or favors with hidden mechanisms that allow him to reverse those benefits when it suits him.

One of the most effective ways he does this is by offering other companies access to Facebook's data, audience, or platform. Startups and competitors are led to believe they are getting a valuable opportunity, only to find that Facebook later alters its terms or changes its algorithms in ways that render their advantage useless.

For example, Facebook allowed third-party apps to deeply integrate with its platform, giving them access to user data and engagement tools. Many companies built their entire businesses around this access, thinking they had won a strategic partnership. Later, Facebook cut off that access, destroying entire companies that had become dependent on it.

Similarly, after acquiring Instagram, Zuckerberg initially allowed it to operate independently, making the founders and users believe that Facebook would not interfere. But as Instagram grew, he gradually eroded its independence, integrating its features and user data into Facebook's ecosystem until it became just another extension of Meta.

These tactics create the illusion that other businesses are securing valuable partnerships, but in reality, Zuckerberg is simply putting them in a position where he can later control or eliminate them.

The High-Anchor Drop –
How Larry Ellison Gets His Desired Terms

Larry Ellison frequently uses extreme initial demands to manipulate negotiations. By starting with an outrageous position, he conditions the other side to feel like they are making progress when he later "compromises."

For example, when negotiating large software contracts, Ellison often begins with pricing that is far above what he actually expects to get. He knows that customers will push back, so he deliberately builds in room to "give up" some of the price. When he eventually agrees to a lower number—one that he intended all along—the customer feels like they have successfully negotiated a better deal.

This tactic plays on a common cognitive bias: people measure success in a negotiation based on where they started rather than the absolute value of the final outcome. By making his initial demand excessively high, Ellison ensures that even after rounds of negotiation, Oracle's contracts remain highly profitable while customers walk away thinking they won a hard-fought battle.

Future Promises Instead of Immediate Cash
— *Ugo Columbo's Real Estate Trick*

Ugo Columbo, one of Miami's most influential real estate developers, frequently structures deals where he appears to give generous financial incentives—but only in the future. This allows him to close deals without actually giving up much at all.

For example, when negotiating with city officials or investors, Columbo often agrees to revenue-sharing deals, future incentives, or additional development rights rather than direct financial payouts. On paper, these concessions seem valuable, but because they are structured as long-term benefits, they often become less meaningful over time.

In some cases, he offers revenue-sharing terms that only activate after a project reaches a certain profit threshold—one that may never actually be met. Other times, he agrees to provide public amenities or affordable housing components, but only after future phases of development, which may never happen.

By the time these future promises are supposed to be fulfilled, the deal's structure has usually shifted, making them easy to renegotiate, delay, or eliminate altogether.

Distraction Concessions —
How Jerry Buss Manipulated Sponsorship Deals

Jerry Buss, the legendary owner of the Los Angeles Lakers, was an expert at giving small, visible concessions to distract from much larger financial victories happening in the background.

When negotiating sponsorship deals, Buss often allowed brands to secure high-profile advertising placements, luxury suite perks, or exclusive partnerships with the Lakers. To sponsors, these benefits seemed significant, and they felt like they were getting an incredible deal.

However, while brands were celebrating their sponsorship perks, Buss ensured that the financial terms of the deals heavily favored the Lakers. In many cases, he negotiated long-term revenue-sharing agreements, strict renewal clauses, and backend financial incentives that were far more valuable than the surface-level perks that sponsors were focused on.

By steering negotiations toward things that sponsors could feel and see—like courtside branding or VIP experiences—Buss kept them from focusing on the financial mechanisms that truly controlled the deal's value.

Case Study:
How Phil Knight Outsmarted Nike's Distributors

Phil Knight, the founder of Nike, built his company into one of the most dominant brands in the world by outmaneuvering distributors who thought they were getting better deals—only to realize later that they had handed Knight complete control over the supply chain. His ability to structure negotiations in a way that provided the illusion of victory to the other side while secretly securing long-term dominance is a masterclass in strategic dealmaking.

Nike's Early Struggles with Distributors

In Nike's early days, the company was not the global powerhouse it is today. Instead, it was a scrappy upstart trying to carve out market share in an industry dominated by established brands like Adidas and Puma. Nike needed distributors to sell its shoes, but these distributors held all the power. They had leverage over which brands to promote, which products to stock, and which companies to prioritize.

Nike's distributors constantly pressured Knight for lower wholesale prices, higher margins, and better contract terms. Many of them were skeptical about Nike's long-term potential and used their leverage to extract as many concessions as possible. They wanted more control over pricing, distribution logistics, and marketing strategies.

The Illusion of Victory –
How Phil Knight Gave Distributors What They Wanted While Taking What He Needed

Instead of outright refusing distributor demands, Knight allowed them to believe they were winning the negotiations. He made concessions that seemed significant on the surface, but in reality, they were structured in a way that secured Nike's long-term control.

- **Lower Wholesale Prices – But Only in Exchange for Exclusive Distribution**
  Agreements Distributors wanted lower prices per unit. Knight agreed—but only if they signed long-term contracts that required them to stock and prioritize Nike products over competitors. Over time, these contracts locked in Nike as their primary supplier, ensuring Nike's market dominance while preventing distributors from easily switching to other brands.

- **Higher Margins for Distributors – While Controlling Their Inventory**
  Distributors demanded better profit margins. Knight agreed—but structured the deal in a way that Nike controlled inventory shipments and product selection. This meant distributors could only sell what Nike provided, giving Nike near-total control over supply and demand. If distributors wanted to continue receiving in-demand shoes, they had to follow Nike's rules.

- **More Marketing Control for Distributors – While Nike Built Direct-to-Consumer Branding**
  In early deals, Nike allowed distributors to have more control over in-store marketing efforts. However, at the same time,

Knight focused heavily on building Nike's direct consumer branding, signing sponsorship deals with athletes like Michael Jordan and leveraging mass media campaigns that bypassed traditional retail marketing. This shift made Nike's brand stronger than the retailers themselves, giving Nike a direct connection with consumers and reducing distributor influence over purchasing decisions.

How Distributors Became Dependent on Nike

At first, distributors believed they had won better deals. They celebrated the fact that they had lower prices, better margins, and more flexibility in their retail strategies. But over time, they realized that the true winner was Phil Knight and Nike.

- Nike's exclusive contracts meant that distributors couldn't easily replace Nike with competing brands, even if they wanted to.

- Nike controlled inventory distribution, meaning retailers had to rely on Nike's supply decisions rather than their own.

- Nike's direct-to-consumer marketing made customers demand Nike products specifically, forcing retailers to stock Nike regardless of the contractual terms.

By the time distributors realized how much power they had conceded, Nike had grown into a dominant force that was too big to challenge. Distributors became completely dependent on Nike's supply, and their previous negotiating power had evaporated.

Nike's Ultimate Move –
Cutting Out Distributors Entirely

Once Nike became an industry giant, Phil Knight took his strategy even further by removing distributors from the equation altogether. With its brand firmly established, Nike shifted towards a direct-to-consumer model, opening its own flagship stores and expanding its e-commerce platform.

This meant that:

- Nike could now sell directly to customers, eliminating the need to negotiate with distributors at all.

- Retailers who once dictated Nike's sales strategy were now at the mercy of Nike's own stores and online platform.

- Nike no longer had to make pricing or margin concessions because customers were coming directly to them.

This was the final stage of Knight's negotiation strategy. He had spent years giving distributors what they thought were victories while quietly making them irrelevant. By the time Nike was ready to remove them, the company was too powerful to stop.

Key Takeaways

- Making the other side feel like they won is often more effective than outright defeating them. When people believe they got a good deal, they are less likely to challenge or renegotiate later. Nike's distributors didn't realize they had lost until it was too late.

- Long-term control is more valuable than short-term profits. Phil Knight structured Nike's agreements so that he gave up minor financial advantages upfront in exchange for strategic control over distribution and brand dominance.

- Reversible concessions allow you to offer temporary benefits that can later be taken away or modified. Nike allowed distributors to set in-store marketing strategies but eventually made them obsolete by building direct consumer relationships.

- Exclusive contracts can be disguised as favors while actually limiting the other party's flexibility. Distributors thought they were getting better pricing, but they were really getting locked into Nike's supply chain.

- Once you make the other side dependent on you, their negotiating power disappears. By controlling inventory and marketing demand, Nike ensured that retailers had no choice but to comply with its terms.

- The ultimate negotiation move is making your counterpart irrelevant. Once Nike had established itself as a global brand, it cut out distributors entirely and took full control over its sales channels.

Final Thought

Phil Knight's genius was not just in designing great shoes— it was in designing great deals. He let distributors think they had won early negotiations while strategically positioning Nike for total control. By the time retailers realized what had happened, they were locked into contracts they could not escape, and Nike had transformed from a struggling shoe company into a global empire.

The best negotiators do not just win at the table. They structure deals so that their victory continues to grow over time— while their counterparts remain unaware until it is too late to do anything about it.

CHAPTER 8:

The Power of Chaos –
Creating Uncertainty to Force Better Terms

Billionaire dealmakers understand that uncertainty breeds desperation. When people feel like they are losing control, they become more willing to accept deals that provide short-term stability—often at a significant long-term cost. Chaos is not just a side effect of high-stakes negotiations; it is a weapon that can be used to weaken opponents, eliminate competition, and create better leverage.

By introducing controlled chaos into a negotiation, elite negotiators force the other side to react emotionally rather than strategically. When a counterparty is scrambling to regain a sense of control, they are far more likely to concede on key terms, lower their demands, or exit a deal entirely.

Tactics for Using Chaos as a Weapon

Blitzkrieg Negotiation –
How Stanley Kroenke Overwhelms His Opponents

Stanley Kroenke, the billionaire owner of the Los Angeles Rams, Arsenal FC, and multiple other sports franchises, is not just a businessman—he is a strategic negotiator who uses speed, legal complexity, and relentless pressure to force outcomes in his favor. His blitzkrieg negotiation strategy overwhelms opponents with a constant barrage of legal filings, zoning maneuvers, media leaks, and financial shifts, leaving them scrambling to react rather than forming an effective counterattack.

By the time the opposition understands what is happening, Kroenke has already moved to the next phase of his plan, forcing them into a defensive and reactionary position. Nowhere was this strategy more evident than in his highly controversial relocation of the Rams from St. Louis to Los Angeles—a move that reshaped the NFL's financial landscape and left city officials, fans, and competing franchises completely blindsided.

How Kroenke Weaponized Chaos to Move the Rams to Los Angeles

In 2016, after years of speculation, Kroenke successfully relocated the St. Louis Rams to Los Angeles, securing an unprecedented deal that gave him complete control over a multi-billion-dollar stadium project and one of the most lucrative media markets in professional sports. However, this move was not a straightforward negotiation—it was a meticulously executed takeover that leveraged legal warfare, financial misdirection, and rapid strategic shifts to ensure there was no way for opponents to stop him in time.

Legal Blitz: Bombarding City Officials With Lawsuits and Zoning Maneuvers

- Kroenke and his legal team launched a multi-pronged legal attack on St. Louis city officials, creating delays, procedural roadblocks, and confusion over the team's obligations to remain in Missouri.

- He strategically manipulated lease agreements with the Edward Jones Dome, where the Rams played, using loopholes and legal challenges to weaken the city's ability to enforce long-term commitments.

- While St. Louis officials were still trying to make sense of the shifting legal landscape, Kroenke had already begun laying the groundwork for his Los Angeles plans.

Media Misdirection: Leaking Conflicting Information to Keep Opponents Off Balance

- Kroenke and his team leaked multiple versions of relocation plans to the press, some suggesting he was still considering staying in St. Louis, while others hinted at alternative locations like San Antonio or London.

- This intentional misinformation kept city officials guessing, making it difficult for them to organize a strong public or legal opposition.

- Competing NFL owners and league officials hesitated to challenge Kroenke's plan because they were uncertain about his real intentions, allowing him to gain a first-mover advantage.

Strategic Speed: Moving Faster Than Opponents Could React

- By the time St. Louis city officials and fans realized Kroenke was fully committed to Los Angeles, he had already secured critical land in Inglewood, California, and obtained zoning approvals for the new stadium site.

- He negotiated directly with Los Angeles city officials in secret, cutting St. Louis out of the discussion entirely and ensuring they had no way to block the move.

- St. Louis was left playing catch-up, scrambling to present a last-minute proposal to keep the Rams, but by then, Kroenke had already built too much momentum toward relocation.

Why Blitzkrieg Negotiation Works

The core principle behind Kroenke's blitzkrieg negotiation style is that opponents cannot organize an effective counterstrategy if they are constantly forced to react to new threats. This approach works because:

- **Speed Kills Resistance** – The faster a negotiator moves, the harder it is for the opposition to create a coordinated response.

St. Louis officials never had enough time to properly challenge Kroenke's moves before he advanced to the next step.

- **Misdirection Creates Hesitation** – By leaking multiple relocation plans and legal challenges, Kroenke forced stakeholders to waste time debating what was real, rather than preparing a unified defense.

- **Legal Complexity Slows Opponents Down** – Even when officials and other owners wanted to stop him, they had to navigate a complex web of legal filings, zoning regulations, and contract disputes—all of which worked in Kroenke's favor.

- **Public Perception Manipulation Weakens Resistance** – By controlling the media narrative, Kroenke ensured that fans, investors, and even competing owners were confused about his true intentions, preventing an organized backlash.

The Final Outcome:
A Billion-Dollar Victory for Kroenke

By the time the relocation was officially approved in January 2016, Kroenke had already won. The NFL owners voted in favor of the move, the Rams left St. Louis, and Kroenke secured one of the most valuable sports franchises in America's second-largest media market.

- The Rams' valuation skyrocketed after the move, making Kroenke billions in increased franchise value.

- His privately funded SoFi Stadium in Inglewood, California, became a centerpiece of NFL media deals, securing long-term profitability.

- St. Louis, despite later winning a lawsuit against the NFL, was left without an NFL team and with no way to undo the damage.

How to Apply Blitzkrieg Negotiation to Business Deals

- Kroenke's method of overwhelming opponents with rapid legal, financial, and strategic shifts is not just for sports moguls—it is a powerful tool in corporate takeovers, real estate deals, and high-stakes business negotiations.

- Move faster than your opponents can react – By the time the other side understands what's happening, they should already be at a disadvantage.

- Create complexity that slows down opposition – Use legal, financial, and contractual maneuvers to force opponents into bureaucratic gridlock.

- Control the media narrative – Misinformation and conflicting reports create confusion, preventing an organized response.

- Ensure no single point of attack – Keep shifting your strategy so that by the time your opponent reacts, the battlefield has changed.

Kroenke's blitzkrieg approach proves that in high-stakes negotiations, speed, misdirection, and relentless pressure can turn even the most controversial and difficult deals into unstoppable victories.

Manufactured Public Pressure –
How Dan Gilbert Uses Media to Shift Negotiations

Dan Gilbert, the billionaire owner of the Cleveland Cavaliers and a major real estate investor, understands the power of leaking half-truths and strategic misinformation to create pressure during negotiations. By controlling public perception, he can steer government officials, competitors, and business partners into making rushed decisions based on fear and urgency.

- When negotiating tax incentives for a new development, Gilbert leaked selective details about the deal's potential failure, causing panic among investors and city officials.

- He created artificial urgency by suggesting that competing cities were offering better terms, making local officials feel like they had to act quickly or lose the project.

- By manipulating media coverage, Gilbert ensured that key stakeholders were pressured into approving favorable terms before they had a chance to fully evaluate the deal.

Public pressure is one of the most powerful weapons in negotiation, and Gilbert has mastered the art of using incomplete but emotionally compelling information to create momentum in his favor.

Making the Deal Feel "Temporary" –
How Ian Schrager Creates Artificial Urgency

Ian Schrager, the legendary hotel developer and co-founder of Studio 54, has mastered the art of using scarcity and exclusivity as psychological triggers to push people into making fast decisions. He understands that when something appears to be available only for a short time, people feel pressure to act quickly before they miss out. This principle applies to his negotiations with investors, city officials, and business partners, where he carefully creates the illusion of urgency, forcing others to agree to his terms before they fully understand the long-term implications.

- **One of Schrager's most effective strategies is framing his hotel deals as "limited-time opportunities."** By making it seem like there is only a short window to invest, he eliminates the possibility of drawn-out negotiations or second-guessing. Investors and city officials feel compelled to commit immediately, fearing that waiting too long will result in missing out on a lucrative deal. This tactic not only speeds up the negotiation process but also prevents potential partners from having the time to conduct deeper due diligence, ultimately giving Schrager an upper hand.

- **Another powerful method Schrager employs is the illusion of competing buyers**. When presenting a deal, he strategically implies that multiple investors or developers are interested, creating a sense of competition. This makes the other party believe they must act quickly or risk losing out to someone else. Even when no other bidders exist, the fear of losing the opportunity forces decision-makers to commit without fully exploring other options. This tactic has allowed Schrager to dictate the terms of his deals while making partners feel like they made the choice themselves.

- **Schrager also understands the importance of maintaining the appearance of flexibility while keeping full control**. In the early stages of negotiations, he often allows his partners to believe they have leverage, offering them what seem to be flexible terms or alternative options. However, once they have committed, those options quietly disappear. By gradually shifting the framework of the deal, he ensures that the final terms are always in his favor. Those who enter negotiations with Schrager believing they have room to negotiate later often find themselves locked into agreements that give him far more control than they initially expected.

This approach ensures that by the time his partners realize what they have conceded, it is too late to back out. They are already financially and strategically invested in the deal, leaving them with no choice but to move forward on Schrager's terms. His ability to create urgency, manipulate perceived competition, and gradually tighten control has made him one of the most successful hotel developers in the world. His method serves as a reminder that in high-stakes negotiations, the illusion of choice and the pressure of time can be just as powerful as financial leverage.

FUD (Fear, Uncertainty, Doubt) –
How BlackRock Uses Market Chaos to Get Better Deals

BlackRock, the world's largest asset manager, is notorious for strategically introducing uncertainty into financial markets to drive down asset prices before making acquisitions. This method, known as FUD (Fear, Uncertainty, Doubt), is used to make distressed sellers accept lower valuations out of fear that their assets will lose even more value.

• Before buying into a struggling industry, BlackRock creates doubt about market stability by releasing reports that highlight risks and potential downturns

• The firm exaggerates regulatory or economic concerns, making competitors hesitate before making counteroffers.

• By the time the market has fully absorbed the negative sentiment, BlackRock steps in to acquire assets at rock-bottom prices, securing massive long-term gains.

This strategy is particularly effective because it preys on fear-based decision-making, forcing sellers into defensive moves that ultimately benefit BlackRock.

Case Study:
How Elon Musk Used Chaos to Buy Twitter

Elon Musk's acquisition of Twitter in 2022 was one of the most chaotic, unpredictable, and masterfully controlled negotiations in corporate history. Unlike traditional buyouts, where buyers conduct due diligence, quietly negotiate, and close the deal smoothly, Musk intentionally introduced uncertainty to destabilize Twitter from within. By weaponizing market reactions, creating public doubt, and forcing Twitter's board into a no-win scenario, he secured the platform for a lower valuation while gaining full control over its future.

At every stage of the deal, Musk kept Twitter's leadership, investors, and employees guessing, leaving them with no stable footing to negotiate from. His approach not only forced Twitter into defensive decision-making, but it also weakened the company's bargaining power so significantly that by the time the deal was finalized, Twitter's only viable option was to surrender to Musk's terms.

Step 1: Announce the Deal, Then Create Doubt

Musk started his acquisition with a bold and aggressive move, publicly announcing his intent to purchase Twitter at a premium price. This forced the Twitter board into a high-pressure situation, as they had to take the offer seriously while navigating shareholder expectations.

- By making his offer public instead of private, Musk immediately shifted leverage in his favor. The board had to respond under intense scrutiny from investors, media, and regulators, limiting their flexibility.

- Within weeks of his announcement, Musk began questioning Twitter's financials, user data, and overall leadership, sowing doubt about the company's stability.

- He claimed Twitter had a massive issue with fake accounts and bots, implying the company had misled investors about its user base. This public accusation created uncertainty around Twitter's actual value, making shareholders nervous.

- By attacking Twitter's integrity in such a high-profile manner, Musk caused a ripple effect where Twitter's perceived worth began to decline, leading to stock price instability.

Instead of following through with a smooth acquisition, Musk used chaos to devalue the asset he was trying to buy, making shareholders desperate for a resolution.

Step 2: Weaponize Market Reactions to Gain More Leverage

Once Musk introduced uncertainty into the deal, Twitter's stock price became highly volatile, causing internal panic among executives and board members. This was a critical moment in Musk's strategy—he let market forces work in his favor, amplifying the pressure on Twitter to close the deal quickly.

- Investors became increasingly nervous about the instability surrounding Twitter. The company had gone from a sought-after platform to a high-risk investment in a matter of weeks.

- Major shareholders began questioning Twitter's ability to remain independent. If Musk backed out of the deal, Twitter's stock could plummet even further, eroding billions in value.

- Executives inside Twitter struggled to maintain internal confidence, as Musk's public criticism led employees to fear mass layoffs, leadership changes, and a total restructuring.

- Internal turmoil spilled into the public sphere, with employees leaking negative stories about the company's declining morale and disorganization, further reinforcing Musk's narrative that Twitter was a failing company.

At this stage, Musk wasn't just negotiating with Twitter's board—he was letting their own shareholders and employees pressure them from within.

Step 3: Force Twitter's Board Into a No-Win Scenario

Musk's chaotic strategy reached its peak when Twitter's board realized that uncertainty was destroying the company faster than they could contain it. They were now trapped in a lose-lose situation:

- If they backed out of the deal, Twitter's stock could collapse even further, and shareholders would revolt against the board for failing to secure a buyout at a premium price.

- If they tried to renegotiate, Musk could walk away entirely, leaving them with a destabilized company and an uncertain future.

- If they moved forward with the sale, they had to do so under Musk's conditions, which had evolved significantly from the original offer.

Sensing their desperation, Musk renegotiated key aspects of the deal to lower his financial exposure:

- He pushed for revised terms, ensuring he had more control over operational decisions post-acquisition.

- He weakened the board's influence, setting himself up as the ultimate decision-maker once the deal was finalized.

- By prolonging the chaos, he ensured that Twitter's leadership would accept his demands just to regain a sense of stability.

By the time the acquisition was completed, Twitter's board was exhausted, its employees were uncertain, and Musk had successfully positioned himself as the only viable solution to restore order.

Why Musk's Chaos Strategy Worked

Musk's approach proved that chaos is a weapon in negotiation. By introducing instability, he forced Twitter's board to prioritize short-term resolution over long-term strategy, leading them to accept his terms.

Unlike traditional buyers, who try to instill confidence in the companies they acquire, Musk did the opposite—he created fear and doubt, then positioned himself as the only person who could fix it.

Key Takeaways

- Chaos forces emotional decision-making. When people feel they are losing control, they will accept terms they would normally reject just to restore order.

- Speed overwhelms opponents. By acting faster than the other side can respond, you can keep them constantly on the defensive, making strategic counterplays impossible.

- Media manipulation can create public pressure. Leaking selective or misleading information can force competitors and officials into rushed decisions.

- Artificial urgency speeds up deals. Making the other side believe a deal is temporary or that they are in direct competition forces them to act before they fully understand the long-term implications.

- FUD (Fear, Uncertainty, Doubt) can lower prices. Introducing uncertainty about market conditions can make sellers accept deals at a discount.

- Controlled unpredictability weakens the other side. When opponents are unsure of what will happen next, they lose their ability to plan effectively, making them more vulnerable to aggressive tactics.

Final Thought

Elon Musk's acquisition of Twitter was not just a business deal—it was a masterclass in using chaos as leverage. By creating uncertainty, manipulating public perception, and destabilizing Twitter from within, he forced the board into a corner where selling to him was their only option.

This strategy is not limited to billion-dollar tech acquisitions. In any high-stakes negotiation, the ability to create and control chaos can break down resistance, weaken the other side's position, and force faster, more favorable decisions. The key is ensuring that by the time your opponent's realize they've been outmaneuvered, the deal is already done on your terms

Cutting Off the Other Side's Options —
The No-Way-Out Strategy

One of the most ruthless and effective tactics in negotiation is systematically eliminating every alternative available to the other party until the only choice left is yours. This strategy forces opponents into a position of dependency, where they are left with no viable exit path and must concede to the terms set by the stronger negotiator.

Billionaires and elite dealmakers use this method to trap competitors, suppliers, employees, and even governments into long-term commitments that heavily favor them. By the time the opposing party realizes their options have disappeared, it is too late to back out, and they have no choice but to comply.

Tactics for Eliminating Alternatives

Controlling Suppliers — *How Michael Dell Blocked Competitors from Sourcing Materials*

Michael Dell built his computer empire not just by innovating technology but by securing exclusive control over supply chains, leaving competitors with limited sourcing options.

- Dell locked in exclusive manufacturing contracts, ensuring that top-tier component suppliers prioritized his company's orders over competitors.

- By securing bulk production deals early, he created scarcity in the market, forcing rival PC makers to pay higher prices or accept inferior components.

- When suppliers were reluctant to sign exclusivity agreements, Dell used financial incentives, stock options, and long-term commitments to ensure they had no reason to work with competitors.

Over time, this approach allowed Dell to control pricing, maintain a cost advantage, and limit the ability of rival companies to scale efficiently.

Locking Up Key Talent — *How Jorge Perez Prevents Competitors from Hiring His Architects and Designers*

Jorge Perez, the Miami-based billionaire real estate developer and founder of The Related Group, understands that world-class architecture and design are critical to the success of luxury real estate projects. In an industry where differentiation is key, Perez has mastered the art of securing top-tier architects and designers, making it nearly impossible for competitors to replicate his signature aesthetic. His strategy involves long-term contracts, exclusive collaboration agreements, and performance-based incentives that ensure loyalty while preventing rival developers from accessing the same creative talent.

Exclusive Contracts for Top-Tier Architects

One of Perez's primary tactics is structuring deals with renowned architects that guarantee them continuous, high-paying work in exchange for exclusivity. These agreements prevent top architectural firms from taking on projects for competing developers, effectively locking down the best talent in the industry. By doing so, he ensures that his properties feature cutting-edge design that cannot be easily replicated elsewhere.

Performance-Based Incentives for Designers

Beyond architects, Perez secures top interior designers and landscape architects by offering performance-based bonuses that incentivize long-term loyalty. These financial rewards are tied to project milestones, sales performance, or aesthetic achievements, ensuring that designers remain committed to The Related Group's portfolio instead of seeking opportunities with rival firms.

Creating an Unmatched Design Monopoly

By monopolizing elite creative professionals, Perez ensures that his developments maintain a distinctive edge. Even if competitors attempt to replicate his style, they cannot hire the same architects and designers responsible for his properties' success. This strategy forces other developers to settle for second-tier talent, making it significantly harder for them to compete in Miami's ultra-competitive luxury real estate market.

A Long-Term Vision for Design Excellence

Perez's approach goes beyond simple contractual obligations—it is part of a broader vision to cement his brand as the leader in high-end real estate development. By continuously working with the best creative minds, he fosters innovation and maintains a design consistency that buyers and investors associate with quality and prestige.

Through these strategic maneuvers, Jorge Perez not only secures the best creative talent but also effectively raises the barrier to entry for competitors, ensuring that The Related Group remains at the forefront of luxury real estate development.

Trapping with Legal Complexity – *How Mark Cuban Forces Startups into Long-Term Commitments*

Mark Cuban, billionaire investor, entrepreneur, and owner of the Dallas Mavericks, has built a reputation not just for his sharp business acumen but also for his ability to structure investment deals that give him long-term leverage over startups. While many investors provide capital with flexible terms, Cuban often constructs intricate legal agreements that make it incredibly difficult for founders to walk away once they accept his money. His approach ensures that he retains control, influence, and financial upside, even if a startup seeks to pivot or attract other investors.

Investment Agreements with Legal Traps

Cuban structures his funding deals with multiple layers of legal conditions that significantly limit a startup's ability to operate freely. These agreements often contain clauses that make it difficult for companies to raise money from other investors without triggering financial penalties or dilution terms that favor him. By doing so, he creates a situation where startups must prioritize his interests over potential competing offers, effectively locking them into long-term financial reliance on his capital.

Strict Non-Compete Clauses to
Prevent Founders from Escaping

One of Cuban's most powerful tools is the inclusion of strict non-compete clauses that restrict founders from pursuing opportunities outside of their startup's original mission. If an entrepreneur attempts to pivot into a new market or launch a different business, they could face financial consequences, such as forfeiting equity or paying back Cuban's investment under unfavorable terms. This strategy prevents founders from walking away and ensures that Cuban's stake in the business remains protected, even if the company struggles or needs to change direction.

Performance-Based Funding
Disbursements to Maintain Control

Instead of providing a lump-sum investment upfront, Cuban often structures deals with performance-based funding disbursements. This means that startups only receive additional capital if they meet specific milestones, which he defines in the agreement. While this approach may seem like a reasonable way to ensure accountability, it also creates a situation where the startup becomes increasingly dependent on his terms to continue operating. Once a company accepts his money, they are often forced to negotiate future funding rounds under his conditions, further strengthening his grip on the business.

Startups Realizing Too Late That They're Trapped

Many early-stage companies, desperate for funding and credibility, accept Cuban's deals without fully grasping the long-term restrictions baked into the legal fine print. By the time founders realize they have limited flexibility to raise alternative capital, shift strategies, or even exit the business without severe consequences, they are already deeply entangled in agreements that favor Cuban.

Through these legal maneuvers, Mark Cuban ensures that his investments are not just financial transactions but long-term strategic plays that give him influence, leverage, and control over startups well beyond the initial funding stage. His approach allows him to dictate the terms of engagement, leaving founders with few options other than to operate within the framework he has carefully constructed.

Regulatory Manipulation –
How Rupert Murdoch Uses Policy to Handcuff Competitors

Rupert Murdoch, the global media tycoon behind Fox and News Corp, has mastered the art of influencing regulatory environments to create advantages for his businesses while limiting competitors.

- Murdoch lobbies for media regulations that disproportionately impact competitors while benefiting his own networks.

- He uses strategic acquisitions to push for rule changes that make it harder for new entrants to gain market share.

- Before making acquisitions, he works behind the scenes to ensure that laws will favor his company post-merger, making it easier to dominate the industry.

By the time competitors realize what has happened, they are already dealing with legal and regulatory barriers that make competing against Murdoch's empire nearly impossible.

Case Study: How Stephen Ross Forced Hudson Yards Tenants Into Long-Term Deals

Stephen Ross, the billionaire developer behind Hudson Yards in New York City, executed one of the most sophisticated no-way-out strategies in commercial real estate history. By systematically removing competing options for major corporate tenants, Ross engineered an environment where businesses had no viable alternative but to commit to his development—on his terms and for decades.

Hudson Yards is now a $25 billion mixed-use mega-development, but its success wasn't guaranteed at the start. The site was initially a complex, unattractive, and highly speculative real estate gamble—a massive undertaking that required extreme foresight, aggressive dealmaking, and long-term financial commitments from blue-chip tenants before construction could even begin. Ross didn't just sell space—he created an ecosystem where corporations felt forced to be part of the development, or risk being left behind in a shifting corporate landscape.

How Ross Eliminated Alternatives
and Created a No-Way-Out Situation for Tenants

Step 1: Position Hudson Yards as the Only Viable Choice for Major Tenants

The biggest challenge in a mega-development like Hudson Yards is securing anchor tenants before the first shovel even hits the ground. Without strong pre-leases, financing becomes difficult, investor confidence wanes, and competing developers can lure tenants elsewhere. Ross knew he had to create a psychological and financial scenario where Hudson Yards wasn't just an option for corporations—it was the only option for those who wanted to remain competitive in Manhattan's evolving corporate scene.

- He strategically framed Hudson Yards as the "future" of Manhattan's business district, leveraging media, political support, and key industry influencers to create momentum.

- He positioned traditional office markets like Midtown East and Downtown as outdated and unable to support the demands of modern corporate tenants.

- He capitalized on growing dissatisfaction with aging office stock in legacy districts, highlighting outdated infrastructure, inefficient layouts, and the lack of cohesive master-planning as key drawbacks.

By framing Hudson Yards as the inevitable next step in Manhattan's corporate evolution, Ross began funneling tenant demand away from traditional office districts, leaving competitors struggling to attract the type of high-profile tenants he was targeting.

Step 2: Use Lease Structuring to Lock in Tenants for Decades

Once Ross positioned Hudson Yards as the must-have address for Fortune 500 companies, he structured lease agreements that ensured tenants couldn't easily leave—or even negotiate terms elsewhere.

- He introduced ultra-long-term lease commitments (15-25 years) as a baseline for anchor tenants. This length ensured that once a corporation committed to Hudson Yards, they weren't just making a short-term real estate decision—they were locking their corporate identity into the district for decades.

- He leveraged complex termination clauses and financial penalties that made relocation impractical. If a tenant wanted to leave, they wouldn't just be breaking a lease—they would be forfeiting massive sunk costs, triggering early termination fees, and in some cases, losing exclusive incentives tied to the Hudson Yards ecosystem.

- He structured rent escalations and participation agreements to ensure ongoing revenue growth. Unlike traditional leases that might cap rental increases at fixed rates, many of the deals Ross negotiated tied future rents to CPI (Consumer Price Index) or overall Hudson Yards performance, ensuring landlords could capture upside in New York's appreciating market.

This strategy eliminated flexibility for corporate tenants, ensuring they had no incentive to look elsewhere once they were in. By the time these tenants realized the full extent of their long-term commitment, Hudson Yards had already become the dominant corporate hub in Manhattan, making it virtually impossible to justify moving elsewhere.

Step 3: Create an Ecosystem Where Leaving Was Not a Rational Choice

Signing a long-term lease is one thing—but Ross ensured that even tenants who considered moving in the future would find it impractical, unnecessary, and financially irresponsible.

- He negotiated massive tax incentives and infrastructure subsidies that were exclusive to Hudson Yards tenants. These benefits created an artificial economic moat around the district—companies that moved elsewhere would immediately lose financial advantages they couldn't replicate in other office markets.

- He structured agreements with retailers, entertainment venues, and hospitality operators to create an integrated business lifestyle experience. Hudson Yards wasn't just an office district—it became a self-contained ecosystem with luxury shopping, Michelin-star dining, elite fitness centers, and entertainment options that made it the most attractive workplace environment in the city.

- He secured commitments from top-tier tenants like Black-Rock, KKR, and Wells Fargo early, creating a domino effect.

Once industry leaders committed to Hudson Yards, competitors and peer firms had little choice but to follow suit or risk being left behind.

Ross essentially removed the option of relocation or second-guessing—once companies moved in, they were embedded in a corporate ecosystem that made it nearly impossible to justify moving out.

Step 4: Force Future Tenants Into an Unequal Bargaining Position

Once the first wave of high-profile corporations had committed to Hudson Yards, Ross leveraged their presence to eliminate negotiation power for future tenants.

- By the time new tenants came looking for space, the most desirable floors and buildings were already occupied. This gave Ross the ability to demand higher rents, stricter lease terms, and fewer concessions from late adopters.

- He structured deals that favored early tenants while making future lease terms even more restrictive. Early tenants benefited from special incentives, while later tenants had to accept higher rates and fewer options.

- He created an environment where major corporations had no leverage to negotiate elsewhere. Any competitor trying to poach tenants from Hudson Yards would have to match a financial and logistical package that was nearly impossible to replicate.

This approach ensured that the power dynamic was always in Ross's favor, allowing him to dictate terms without fear of major corporate tenants leaving or negotiating downward pressure on rents.

The Final Outcome:
A Billion-Dollar Masterclass in Controlling Corporate Real Estate Decisions

By the time companies realized how restrictive their agreements were, Hudson Yards had already become the most desirable business district in New York, and their only option was to stay.

- Ross transformed a speculative mega-development into a corporate must-have. Companies that failed to establish a presence in Hudson Yards risked being seen as lagging behind competitors.

- He structured deals so that even if a tenant wanted to leave, the financial and strategic penalties made it nearly impossible.

- He eliminated competitive alternatives by making Hudson Yards the only logical choice for modern office space in Manhattan.

This was not just a real estate play—it was a strategic takeover of Manhattan's corporate leasing landscape, ensuring that for the next 25 years, the highest-value tenants would remain in his development, creating a stable, appreciating asset portfolio with unparalleled financial upside.

Key Takeaways
for Elite Commercial Real Estate Professionals

- The most valuable real estate is not just a physical location—it's a controlled ecosystem where tenants feel they have no alternative but to be there.

- Long-term lease structuring should not just lock in tenants but make leaving so financially painful that they won't even consider it.

- Creating artificial exclusivity forces corporations into a psychological and strategic commitment before they even sign a lease.

- The best deals are secured before tenants even realize they are being strategically boxed into a no-way-out scenario.

- If your development is positioned correctly, future tenants will have no leverage to negotiate against you, ensuring maximum profitability.

Final Thought

Stephen Ross didn't just build Hudson Yards—he designed a system that made it impossible for corporations to say no. His approach demonstrates that in high-stakes commercial real estate, the true game is not just about attracting tenants—it's about eliminating every other option until the only rational decision is the one you control.

Key Takeaways

- Controlling supply chains can eliminate competitors before they even have a chance to scale. If they cannot access quality materials or suppliers, they are forced to operate at a disadvantage.

- Locking up top talent ensures that competitors cannot replicate your success. If they cannot hire the best, they are always playing with second-tier resources.

- Legal complexity can trap partners and competitors into long-term agreements that benefit you indefinitely. If the deal is structured correctly, they will have no choice but to comply.

- Influencing regulations before making acquisitions can guarantee that your deal will face no obstacles while competitors struggle under new rules.

- Forcing long-term commitments from key players in an industry can create a self-reinforcing advantage, where everyone else must follow your lead.

CHAPTER 10:

The Billionaire's Endgame –
Winning Before the Other Side Even Starts

At the highest levels of power, success isn't about reacting—it's about engineering a landscape where the game is already won before the competition even realizes they're playing. The world's most successful billionaires don't just dominate industries; they structure them in ways that make their victory inevitable.

This level of strategic dominance isn't about being the best at responding to competition—it's about ensuring competition never gets the chance to respond at all. By controlling key economic infrastructure, monopolizing markets before others can, shaping regulatory environments, and forcing competitors into unwinnable battles, these titans secure their positions long before anyone else can challenge them.

Tactics for Pre-Determining the Winner

Building the Economic Infrastructure –
Stanley Kroenke Ensured His Los Angeles Stadium Would Be the Only Viable NFL Relocation Option

When billionaire sports mogul Stanley Kroenke decided to bring an NFL team to Los Angeles, he didn't just lobby for a team to move—he engineered the only possible outcome that would make relocation inevitable on his terms.

- **Land Acquisition Before the Market Knew** – Years before any formal NFL relocation discussions, Kroenke secretly purchased a massive 298-acre plot in Inglewood, California. By the time the public and other NFL owners realized what he was doing, he already controlled the best possible location for an NFL stadium in Los Angeles.

- **Privately Funded Stadium to Remove Approval Hurdles** – Unlike other proposals that required public funding and lengthy approval processes, Kroenke structured his project to be privately financed, eliminating the biggest argument against it.

- **Creating a Revenue Ecosystem Around the Stadium** – Kroenke didn't just build a stadium; he developed an entire entertainment district, ensuring that his investment would dominate the local economy and make it impossible for competitors to build anything comparable.

By the time other NFL owners considered relocating teams, Kroenke's stadium was the only realistic option—forcing the league to accept his terms and making him the most powerful team owner in the process.

Pre-Securing Market Monopoly –
Bill Gates Made Microsoft Software an Industry Standard Before Competitors Could Respond

Bill Gates didn't approach competition with the mindset of simply being better—he ensured that his rivals never had a fair chance to compete in the first place. Instead of waiting for the software industry to evolve naturally, he structured Microsoft's strategy in a way that made it the foundation of the computing world before serious competitors could even establish themselves. His approach wasn't about winning market share in an open battle; it was about creating an ecosystem so dominant that competing against Microsoft was an exercise in futility.

Gates understood early on that in the emerging personal computer (PC) revolution, the operating system wasn't just another
piece of software—it was the control point for everything else.
If he could position Microsoft as the default operating system
provider before alternatives gained traction, he wouldn't have
to fight for dominance—he would already own the battlefield.

Preloading Microsoft on Every PC

One of Gates' most powerful strategies was striking exclusive deals with PC manufacturers to make Microsoft's operating
system the default option. In the early days of personal computing, multiple companies were competing to establish their
operating systems as the industry standard, but Gates moved
quickly to ensure that Windows became the only viable choice
for mass adoption.

- **The IBM Partnership** – Gates secured a pivotal deal with IBM
  in the 1980s to provide the operating system for their first
  personal computers. This decision alone set Microsoft on a
  path to dominance, as IBM was the most respected name in
  computing at the time.

- **Bundling Windows with Hardware Manufacturers** – Microsoft didn't just supply IBM—Gates **expanded these exclusive
  deals** to other major PC makers, ensuring that Windows came
  pre-installed on nearly every computer being sold.

- **Eliminating Choice at the Consumer Level** – By the time
  competitors like Apple or independent software makers tried
  to offer alternatives, Microsoft had already become the default
  option on almost every PC. Consumers were buying computers with Windows already built in, making alternative systems
  an uphill battle.

This tactic ensured that, from the moment personal computers
became mainstream, Microsoft was already embedded into the
industry's DNA, leaving competitors scrambling to find a foothold.

Licensing Deals That Created Dependence

Unlike other software companies that might have tried to sell an operating system outright, Gates structured Microsoft's business around **licensing agreements**, a strategy that gave Microsoft control long after a sale was made.

- **Recurring Revenue Model** – Instead of making one-time sales, Microsoft licensed Windows to manufacturers and businesses, ensuring continuous revenue streams and creating **ongoing dependence** on Microsoft products.

- **Locking in Corporate Users** – Microsoft made sure that once a business adopted its software, switching to a different system would be a logistical nightmare. Companies that built their operations around Microsoft's ecosystem—Windows, MS-DOS, and later Office—found it increasingly **expensive and disruptive** to migrate to anything else.

- **Licensing Restrictions That Blocked Competition** – Microsoft's agreements with manufacturers often prohibited them from pre-installing competing operating systems or charged penalties for using alternatives, effectively eliminating rival software before it even had a chance to gain market share.

By making Microsoft's software a **long-term dependency** rather than a one-time purchase, Gates ensured that companies, governments, and individuals **stayed locked into his ecosystem**, whether they liked it or not.

Forcing Industry Standardization

Beyond just securing distribution, Gates **engineered an entire industry structure** where Microsoft became the standard for business and consumer computing. Once Windows reached critical mass, it wasn't just the dominant system—it was the expected default.

- **Creating Compatibility as a Weapon** – Microsoft ensured that its software and operating system worked seamlessly with major business applications and enterprise systems. If a competitor introduced an alternative OS, it wouldn't work with essential Microsoft programs, making adoption difficult.

- **Encouraging Third-Party Developers to Build on Windows** – Gates leveraged Microsoft's dominance to convince software developers that writing programs for Windows was the only financially viable choice. This created a network effect where most new software was built for Windows first, further cementing its position as the industry's default.

- **Making Microsoft Office the Only Logical Choice** – By developing a suite of productivity tools (Word, Excel, PowerPoint, etc.) that integrated perfectly with Windows, Microsoft made it nearly impossible for businesses to justify switching to alternative systems. Even if they preferred a different operating system, they couldn't afford to abandon Microsoft Office, reinforcing Microsoft's dominance across the software landscape.

Once Microsoft had successfully set its software as the industry standard, **switching costs became too high** for businesses and individuals alike. By the time competitors like Apple, Linux, or other independent software firms tried to break in, they weren't just competing against Microsoft's products—they were **competing against an entire ecosystem** that Microsoft had already entrenched in the global market.

The End Result: Too Big to Displace

Gates didn't just build a dominant software company—he architected a monopoly that made Microsoft's continued dominance inevitable.

- Competitors were shut out before they could gain traction.

- Businesses and governments became financially dependent on Microsoft products.

- The software industry was forced to align with Microsoft as the default standard.

By the time regulators and competitors realized what had happened, Microsoft was too deeply embedded into global computing to be easily removed. Even lawsuits and antitrust cases against the company couldn't fully unwind the market position Gates had built.

This strategy turned Microsoft into one of the most powerful tech companies in history, not because it had the best technology at every turn, but because Gates structured the industry in a way that ensured Microsoft was always in control before others could respond

Controlling the Legal Playing Field –
Blackstone Sets Up Regulatory Barriers Before Entering New Markets

Private equity giant Blackstone doesn't just look for investment opportunities—it structures legal environments to ensure its dominance before making a move.

- **Influencing Regulations Before Entering a Market** – Before Blackstone invests in a new industry or region, it lobbies for laws and regulations that create barriers to entry for competitors while favoring its own strategies.

- **Strategic Use of Zoning and Land Use Laws** – In real estate, Blackstone often acquires properties before local governments change zoning laws, ensuring that its projects have a competitive advantage while other developers are stuck in red tape.

- **Buying Debt to Control Industries Indirectly** – In many cases, Blackstone doesn't buy companies outright—it buys their debt, giving it leverage over how industries operate without directly owning them.

By the time Blackstone officially enters a market, it has already set the rules in its favor, making it nearly impossible for competitors to succeed.

Forcing Competitors Into the Wrong Fights
— *Mark Zuckerberg Buys Up Potential Threats Early, Preventing Competition Before It Exists*

Mark Zuckerberg doesn't wait for competitors to challenge Facebook—he eliminates them before they become a threat.

- **Acquiring Potential Disruptors Early** – Facebook's purchases of Instagram and WhatsApp weren't just about expanding its empire; they were about preventing future competitors from growing into real threats.

- **Copying Features to Undercut Rivals** – When Zuckerberg couldn't buy Snapchat, he cloned its core features (like Stories) and integrated them into Instagram, making Snapchat's unique selling points irrelevant.

- **Leveraging Facebook's Network Effect** – By ensuring that Facebook and its platforms remain the dominant social networks, Zuckerberg makes it difficult for new entrants to gain traction, forcing them to operate on the fringes of the market.

Rather than competing in a fair fight, Zuckerberg ensures that challengers never get a chance to rise to his level in the first place.

Case Study:
Donald Trump's High-Stakes Negotiation for the Wollman Rink

One of Donald Trump's most remarkable negotiations came in the 1980s when he took over the stalled Wollman Rink renovation in New York City. The project, which had been an embarrassment for the city, became a masterclass in negotiation, public relations, and strategic positioning.

The Problem: A Six-Year Government Failure

By the early 1980s, New York City had been trying—and failing—to renovate Wollman Rink, a beloved public ice-skating rink in Central Park. The renovation, which was supposed to take two years and cost $9 million, had dragged on for six years and ballooned to over $12 million, with no end in sight.

The project had become a symbol of government inefficiency and waste, with city officials unable to solve fundamental problems in construction and refrigeration. As public frustration grew, Trump saw an opportunity to step in—not just to fix the rink, but to negotiate a deal that would make him look like a hero and strengthen his influence in New York politics and real estate.

Trump's Strategic Negotiation Approach

Rather than simply offering to help, Trump positioned himself as the only person who could solve the crisis, forcing the city into a deal that would put him in control under highly favorable terms.

- **Using Public Outrage as Leverage**

  Trump carefully manipulated public perception by highlighting how incompetent the city was in handling the project. He went on a media blitz, repeatedly calling out the city for its failure, making it clear that he could do better. By putting political pressure on officials, he made it almost impossible for them to reject his proposal.

- **Offering a No-Risk Deal for the City**

  Trump proposed that he would complete the rink using his own money—but with the condition that he would manage it once it was completed. This was a strategic move. If the city said no, it would look even more incompetent; if it said yes, Trump would gain public favor and secure a long-term revenue stream from managing the rink.

- **Demanding Complete Control and a Fast Timeline**

  Trump's confidence in his ability to solve the problem was central to his negotiation. He demanded full control over construction and guaranteed that he would finish the project within six months, a timeline that seemed impossible given the city's six-year failure.

- **Forcing the City into a No-Win Situation**

  By positioning himself as the only viable solution, Trump made it politically and practically difficult for the city to refuse his offer. If officials rejected him and the project remained unfinished, they would face public backlash. If they accepted, Trump would gain a massive win—not just in business but in his public image as a bold problem-solver.

The Outcome: Delivering Ahead of Schedule and Under Budget

Once Trump took over, he moved aggressively, hiring a private construction team and bypassing bureaucratic red tape that had slowed the city's progress. The results were undeniable:

- Project completed in just four months instead of the six years the city had wasted.

- Final cost: $2.25 million, a fraction of the city's $12 million failure.

- Trump gained management rights to the rink, turning it into a profitable venture for his company.

- His reputation as a master negotiator and dealmaker was further solidified, giving him increased credibility for future real estate and political ambitions.

Why This Negotiation Was a Masterstroke

Trump's takeover of Wollman Rink was more than just a construction success—it was a textbook example of high-stakes negotiation where he:

- Created leverage by highlighting the city's incompetence and making himself the only logical solution.

- Forced officials into a deal they couldn't refuse by making the decision politically unavoidable.

- Structured the terms in his favor, ensuring he controlled the outcome while the city took all the risk.

- Used the victory to boost his brand and influence, cementing his image as a businessman who could get things done where governments failed.

This case is a prime example of winning before the other side even realizes they're in a negotiation—the essence of billionaire deal-making strategy.

CHAPTER 11:

The Dead Deal Revival –
Resurrecting a Lost Opportunity and Turning It Into a Win

M ost people walk away from a deal once it falls apart, but billionaire negotiators know that dead deals can be the most profitable deals—if you know how to resurrect them.

The ability to bring a failed negotiation back to life on your terms is an advanced power move. It takes patience, strategy, and the ability to manipulate circumstances so that by the time the other side is ready to talk again, they are more desperate, have fewer options, and are willing to accept the deal you originally wanted.

Why the Dead Deal Revival Strategy Works

The Dead Deal Revival Strategy is rooted in timing, psychology, and leverage. While most people see a failed negotiation as the end of the road, billionaire dealmakers understand that a deal is only truly dead when everyone stops wanting it. The key is to recognize that time and circumstances change everything.

By letting the other side walk away, you create an opportunity for them to experience the consequences of losing the deal, making them more open to coming back—but on your terms. Here's why this strategy is so effective:

- **People Panic When a Deal Falls Apart**

When a negotiation collapses, both sides feel a sense of loss, but one side typically needs the deal more. The problem is, in the moment, ego and emotions take over. If you push too hard to keep the deal alive, you appear desperate, and the other party may try to extract more from you.

The key is to let them sit with the decision. Once the initial rush of ego fades, reality sets in.

▷ The other party starts questioning if they made a mistake.

▷ Their team begins second-guessing their decision.

▷ External pressures—financial, competitive, or operational—begin to weigh on them.

▷ Their fear of missing out on a good deal starts creeping in.

At this moment, they start rethinking their position—and that's when you hold all the power.

- **Time Changes the Leverage**

The biggest advantage of walking away from a deal strategically is that time has a way of flipping the leverage in your favor.

▷ **Markets shift** – A competitor who was ready to step in may disappear. Industry conditions may change, making your original offer look better in hindsight.

▷ **Their financial situation may worsen** – If they rejected your offer because they thought they could get a better deal, time might prove them wrong. A cash crunch, a change in funding sources, or unforeseen expenses can make them reconsider.

▷ **Opportunities vanish** – If they had another option on the table, but that deal fell through, they are suddenly left with nothing.

▷ **External forces apply pressure** – Investors, board members, partners, or even customers can push them back toward the deal they previously dismissed.

This shift in leverage makes them far more flexible when they come back to the table.

- **The Other Side Becomes Emotionally Invested**

Once someone commits mentally to a deal, walking away leaves an emotional void.

Even if they initially reject your offer, the idea of the deal still lingers in their mind. If it was something they truly wanted—or if they put in time, effort, and resources into considering it—walking away creates a sense of loss.

This is basic human psychology:

▷ People don't like to lose things they were emotionally attached to.

▷ The more effort they put into considering the deal, the harder it is for them to let go.

▷ Regret sets in over time, especially if the alternatives they hoped for don't materialize.

By walking away and remaining calm, you create a situation where they eventually convince themselves that they want the deal again.

And when they come back? They are already softened up for renegotiation.

- **You Can Rewrite the Rules**

A revived deal is never the same deal. When the other side comes back, you are no longer operating under the old negotiation framework.

This is where you exert total control:

▷ You can adjust the terms to make the deal more favorable for you.

▷ You can remove or add new conditions that give you more protection.

▷ You can frame the revived deal as a "compromise", even if it's the same deal you wanted all along.

▷ You can increase the price or change financial terms, citing "new developments" since the original negotiation.

By strategically stalling and letting desperation build on the other side, you set the stage for a better deal—one where you dictate the terms

How Billionaires Revive Dead Deals on Their Terms

The Soft Exit –
Letting the Other Side Think They Won

When a deal collapses, don't fight to save it—let it die in a way that leaves the door open.

• Instead of arguing, say: *"I respect your position, and I understand this deal isn't right at this time. If things change, my door is always open."*

• This **removes hostility** and ensures that when they do reconsider, **they come back to you—on your terms.**

Example: How Carl Icahn Walked Away from Apple—Then Came Back Stronger

Carl Icahn, the billionaire activist investor, pushed for Apple to issue stock buybacks in 2013. When Apple resisted, he publicly backed off, making it seem like he was moving on.

But behind the scenes, he was buying more Apple stock at lower prices. A year later, Apple finally announced a $90 billion buyback—exactly what Icahn wanted.

By pretending to accept the loss, he allowed time and pressure to force Apple into making the decision he wanted—without him having to fight for it.

The Controlled Collapse –
Killing the Deal Strategically

Sometimes, **you have to kill the deal yourself**—but in a way that ensures you can revive it later.

- Create a fake dealbreaker that seems logical but is actually just a waiting game.

- Example: *"The market conditions aren't right, but let's reconnect in six months."*

- This lets you step away without burning bridges while forcing the other side to wait.

EXAMPLE: How Douglas Durst Let a Manhattan Tower Deal Collapse—Then Took Control

Douglas Durst, head of The Durst Organization and one of New York City's most powerful real estate developers, has built an empire by mastering the art of timing, leverage, and strategic patience. One of his most calculated moves involved a high-profile office tower development in Midtown Manhattan, where he allowed a deal to collapse, only to later revive it under terms that gave him full control.

This is a textbook example of the Dead Deal Revival Strategy, where a savvy negotiator lets a deal fall apart—either by walking away or allowing a competitor to fail—before stepping in at the perfect moment to secure it under better conditions.

The Initial Bidding War and Collapse

In the early 2000s, a prime development site near Bryant Park came onto the market. The opportunity to build a new office tower in one of Manhattan's most desirable locations attracted multiple competing developers, including The Durst Organization.

Real estate in Midtown Manhattan is always competitive, and at the time, the economy was booming. Developers were willing to outbid each other aggressively, driving up prices beyond what made financial sense.

Durst was interested in the site, but rather than engaging in an all-out bidding war, he carefully analyzed the risks. He saw what others did not: the warning signs of an overheated market.

Ultimately, another developer won the bid by offering well above what Durst believed was a sustainable price. While others saw this as a loss for Durst, he viewed it as a calculated retreat.

He knew that:

- The winning bidder had structured the deal with high debt leverage, making the project vulnerable to any market downturn.

- The cost of borrowing was increasing, and if interest rates moved higher, financing the project could become problematic.

- The developer was assuming strong demand for office space, but if the market shifted, their leasing projections would be in serious trouble.

Rather than overpay and overextend himself, Durst stepped aside and let the winning bidder **take on all the risk.**

The Market Collapses— And Durst's Prediction Comes True

Just a few years later, the 2008 financial crisis hit.

Commercial real estate development froze across New York City. Lenders pulled back, office demand stalled, and construction costs skyrocketed.

The developer who had won the site suddenly found themselves in serious trouble.

- They had borrowed heavily, but now financing had dried up.

- The projected demand for office space plummeted, making pre-leasing nearly impossible.

- Their construction costs, which were manageable before the crash, became unsustainable with the new economic reality.

With no viable path forward, the developer was forced to abandon the project, losing millions in the process.

As expected, the site went into distress—a situation Durst had anticipated when he first walked away.

Waiting for the Right Moment to Strike

While others saw a dead deal, Durst saw an opportunity. Instead of immediately jumping in, he waited as:

- The previous developer's lenders scrambled to recover their losses.

- The market gradually stabilized, bringing financing options back.

- Property values dropped, making the site far cheaper than when it first went up for bid.

By the early 2010s, the site was back on the market—**but this time, the terms were completely different.**

- The original developer had absorbed the high initial costs and the loss, meaning Durst could step in at a fraction of the original price.

- The zoning approvals, environmental impact reports, and regulatory hurdles had **already been handled**—all thanks to the prior developer's failed attempt.

- The banks and investors, eager to offload the distressed asset, **offered far more favorable financing terms** than those available during the bidding war years earlier.

When Durst finally stepped in, he acquired the property at a massive discount, under financing conditions far superior to what the previous developer had.

Reviving the Project—On His Terms

Once Durst secured the site, he redesigned the project with a more efficient structure, capitalizing on the city's recovery while avoiding the mistakes of his predecessor.

- Instead of speculatively building and hoping to lease later, he secured pre-leases from major corporate tenants before construction even began.

- He leveraged his deep financial connections to structure a deal where construction costs were better managed.

- He revised the building's design to align with evolving tenant needs, making it more attractive than if it had been developed under the original plan.

What had once been a failed deal became one of the most valuable office towers in his portfolio.

Why This Was a Masterclass in the Dead Deal Revival Strategy

Durst played the long game and won by letting his competition make all the mistakes first.

- He didn't overpay in a heated bidding war. He let another developer take the risk, knowing they were overextending themselves.

- The market collapse reversed the power dynamic. When the original developer failed, Durst gained control at a fraction of the cost.

- He secured better financing. The original deal required aggressive leverage, but when Durst stepped in later, banks were eager to lend to a more stable developer.

- He let others absorb the early costs. The zoning approvals, planning, and legal processes had already been handled, streamlining Durst's path to construction.

The Desperation Play –
Letting the Other Side Suffer Before Reviving the Deal

Most people think time kills deals, but time actually increases desperation.

If the other party rejected your offer, let them suffer for a while.

- Watch for signs of financial pressure or industry changes that make them regret rejecting your deal.

- Let them reach out first, but when they do, make them think you've moved on.

- This makes them feel like they must "earn" their way back into the deal—on your terms.

Example: How SoftBank Let WeWork Collapse Before Buying It for Pennies

In 2019, WeWork was valued at $47 billion and trying to go public. SoftBank, a major investor, offered to buy more shares to save the company, but WeWork's leadership refused.
So SoftBank did nothing.
- WeWork's IPO failed spectacularly
- The company's valuation collapsed to $8 billion
- WeWork's CEO was forced out in disgrace
Once the company was in total crisis, SoftBank came back in and bought controlling shares at a fraction of the original price.
By waiting for desperation to set in, SoftBank revived the deal—but at a massive discount.

How to Use the Dead Deal
Revival Strategy in Your Own Negotiations

Let the Other Side Feel the Pain of Losing the Deal

If they walk away, do nothing. Let time, market conditions, and financial stress make them second-guess their decision.

- Keep tabs on their situation—watch for signs they need the deal again.

- When they reach out, act indifferent—this makes them want it more.

2. Create Fake Barriers to Buy Time

If you know a deal isn't working for you, stall with a believable excuse so you can return later with more leverage.

- Example: "We love the deal, but we're overextended this quarter. Let's revisit in six months."

- This buys time for the other side to feel pressure and rethink their position.

3. Reframe the Deal So It Feels Like a "New" Opportunity

A revived deal should never look like the same deal. It needs to feel like a fresh opportunity.

- Change the terms slightly so they think they're getting something better (even if they're not).

- Bring in a new partner, angle, or reason to re-engage.

Example: If a buyer walked away from a real estate deal, re-package it with a "new financing option" or "exclusive opportunity"—even if nothing actually changed.

4. Use External Events to Justify a Comeback

If time has passed, use external factors as the reason for re-opening negotiations—this keeps you from looking desperate.

- Example: "Given recent market shifts, I wanted to check in and see if it makes sense to revisit this."

- This makes it seem like you're doing them a favor, not the other way around.

Final Thought: The Best Deals Are Often the Ones That Almost Didn't Happen

Most people quit when a deal falls apart. Billionaires know that's when the real negotiation begins.

By waiting, repositioning, and reviving deals only when the other side is weaker, they turn losses into victories—and get what they wanted all along, on even better terms.

The next time a deal collapses, don't see it as a failure. See it as an opportunity waiting to be revived—on your terms

In Closing

After 35 years of being in the trenches—studying, researching, and, most importantly, executing these tactics in the real world—I've finally laid it all out for you. This is not a book. This is a weapon. A weapon that, if you dare to wield it, will change how you negotiate, how you sell, and how you dominate any deal that crosses your path.

This is the playbook of the world's most ruthless dealmakers—the billionaires, the corporate raiders, the Wall Street killers who bend reality to their will and leave their opponents in the dust. These aren't theories. These aren't ideas that might work. Every single strategy in this book has been used in billion-dollar negotiations to crush the competition and come out on top.

Now it's your turn.

You now hold the blueprint to control any room, dismantle any resistance, and force your terms onto the table. Whether you're closing a high-stakes real estate deal, securing funding for a massive business venture, or just sharpening your ability to make people move the way you want them to move, this book gives you the edge that 99% of negotiators will never have.

The world isn't fair. But the best negotiators don't play fair—they play to win.

Now you have their secrets.

Go out there. Dominate. Control. Win. And as Tom Brady says "LETS #$%^&* GO"!!!!!!

Mark McClure

www.ingramcontent.com/pod-product-compliance
Lightning Source LLC
Chambersburg PA
CBHW071417210326
41597CB00020B/3542